Praise for

the dogs who found me

"Ken Foster's new memoir, *The Dogs Who Found Me,* is a tale of love and survival—through 9/11, through a near-fatal heart problem, through Hurricane Katrina. . . . It's a memoir that will appeal to dog-lovers, for sure, but it's also a human story of considerable dimensions, framed by national tragedies . . ."

—*The New Orleans Times-Picayune*

"(Foster is) matter-of-fact, sometimes angry, always open-hearted and often full of wonder. . . . At the core of it, this is a book about living a decent life and taking care along the way. You don't have to rescue stray pit bulls to know how important that is."

—*The Oregonian*

". . . [a] beautiful and funny account of dog love. . . . This light, deeply felt chronicle puts that best-selling confection *Marley & Me* in the shade."

—*The Plain Dealer*

"Foster's book might sound dangerously warm and fuzzy, but it maintains an edge of wisdom and self-awareness. . . . Foster has led an untidy life, and he's lucky his pets have taught him the value of letting things get messy."

— Sarah Goodyear, *Time Out New York*

"Generosity and gratitude power this compelling account of the reciprocal nature of rescue. Ken Foster illuminates a profound lesson about saving a life: Doing it makes you able to do it."

—Amy Hempel,
author of *The Collected Stories of Amy Hempel*

"I read this at once, and could hardly bear to put it down. This is a wonderful, strange book, beautiful and funny and moving. It delivers something crucial about bravery, the human spirit, and the place that dogs occupy in our landscapes. It's about confronting need, vulnerability and love, and responding."

—Roxana Robinson,
author of *Sparta* and *Georgia O'Keefe: A Life*

"Pitbulls pitbulls pitbulls, and a man, like me, who loves them. Alternately brutal and sentimental, like the lives of the dogs he rescues. A very very cool book."

—James Frey,
author of *Bright Shiny Morning* and *A Million Little Pieces*

the dogs who found me

what i've learned from pets who were left behind

updated edition

Ken Foster

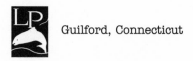

Guilford, Connecticut

An imprint of Rowman & Littlefield

Distributed by NATIONAL BOOK NETWORK

Copyright © 2006 by Ken Foster
First Lyons Press updated paperback edition, 2016

Designed by Sheryl P. Kober

"Her Grave" reprinted from *New and Selected Poems* by Mary Oliver
Copyright ©1992 by Mary Oliver
Reprinted by permission of Beacon Press, Boston

British Library Cataloguing in Publication Information Available

Library of Congress has previously catalogued an earlier (paperback) edition as follows:

Foster, Ken. The dogs who found me : what I've learned from pets who were left behind /
Ken Foster. p. cm.
ISBN 1-59228-749-2
1. Dogs–Anecdotes. 2. Feral dogs–Anecdotes. 3. Foster, Ken. I. Title.
SF426.2F663 2006
636.7–dc22
2005028464

ISBN 978-1-4930-1767-6 (pbk.)
ISBN 978-1-4930-2761-3 (e-book)

♾™ The paper used in this publication meets the minimum requirements of
American National Standard for Information Sciences—Permanence of Paper for
Printed Library Materials, ANSI/NISO Z39.48-1992.

for my friends

A dog comes to you and lives with you in your own house, but you do not therefore own her, as you do not own the rain, or the trees, or the laws which pertain to them . . .

A dog can never tell you what she knows from the
smells of the world, but you know, watching her, that you know
almost nothing . . .

—From "Her Grave"

by Mary Oliver

contents

foreword

"YOU SHOULD WRITE A BOOK ABOUT RESCUING DOGS."

This was my friend and editor Ann Treistman's idea, because it seemed that every time we spoke on the phone, I had a new stray dog staying temporarily in another room and distracting me from our conversation. I thought it was an awful idea. I didn't really know anything about rescuing dogs. I just did it. I'd find a dog running loose, bring him home, and then figure out what to do next. How do I find the owner? How do I find a home? How do I know which organizations to go to for advice? And also: why do people like Ann think this is unusual or interesting?

Part of what was interesting, I realized, was that I hadn't always been this way. I hadn't been a dog person at all. Or, perhaps, I was a closeted dog lover. I began to think that maybe there was a book in this after all, if I could find a way of unearthing that mystery of how I had transformed. But there was still one caveat: "If I write this book, we have to agree that it will be from the point of view of someone who doesn't know what he is doing." I had no interest in trying to pass myself off as an expert on anything, but wondered at what inspired me to overcome my lack of experience to dive headfirst into the lives of these stray dogs, whose endings hadn't yet been determined. If I could find a way to articulate that experience, then I might really have a book.

As I set to writing, two things happened that changed the text and my own life. First, I ended up in the hospital with a heart arrhythmia, and then I moved to New Orleans just before the levee failures left thousands of people and animals struggling to survive. Being helpless is never a comfortable feeling. Accepting help is never easy. But this reversal of fortune resonated with me, informed my own sense of compassion, and deepened my bond with my own dogs, who supported me in ways that go beyond actions and words.

From the beginning, it was important to me that my pit bull Sula be on the cover of the book. She, more than any of my other pets, truly found me one day and walked into my life to stay. It would be strange to have another dog on the cover. I arranged for a photo shoot with Cami Johnson, and the image of Sula peering around the column of a New Orleans porch was perfect. But in the months just before publication, I learned that there was talk of changing the photo. My editor called and said, "You can say no, but I promised to run this idea by you . . ."

I guessed the rest. "They want to use a dog floating in flood water? Absolutely not."

When the book came out and I began to do signings in bookstores, a curious thing happened: there were people there waiting for me. This doesn't typically happen early on in a book tour. There had been no reviews. The print run was the smallest I'd ever been given: under 2,000 copies. So I asked people what brought them to the events. Invariably, the answer was this: "The dog on the cover looks like my dog, and I've never seen a dog like that on a book cover before."

The first print run ran out immediately. And so did the following reprint. Then reviews started coming in, and interviews, including one with Terry Gross on NPR's *Fresh Air*. The reprints continued—no matter how many had been printed, we were still out of stock. It wasn't just the cover photo that people identified with; it was also the experience of falling in love with dogs and investing in their rescue, even when we don't always know what we are doing.

Though *The Dogs Who Found Me* is really just about dogs, a lot of those dogs are what are known as "pit bulls." One of the things I hoped to do was show that they are, in fact, individual personalities more than just a stereotype of a dog. As I toured and met more pit bull owners and animal caretakers who loved the breed, I felt compelled to do something more. In 2008, just before my mother passed away, I got together with a group of people in New Orleans and formed The Sula Foundation in New Orleans. It seemed illogical at the time that there were no other pit bull organizations in the city, although pit bulls made up most of the dogs. We worked with area shelters and did fostering in a limited way while focusing on community outreach, with low-cost vaccination clinics and training and free spay/neuter services. I hoped, too, to write a pit bull-specific book, since it seemed clear that there was a market of readers waiting for such a thing. This took longer. Publishers told me their staffs would quit if they published a book about pit bulls; this struck me as ridiculously melodramatic. Finally, in 2012, I published *I'm a Good Dog: Pit Bulls, America's Most Beautiful and Misunderstood Pet*, and it immediately sold out its first printing.

• • •

It's an incredible honor that people are still reading this book ten years later. It may have turned out quite differently if I had known how widely read it would become. I may have been more self-conscious in the way I portrayed things; I may have been less honest with my feelings at the time. But that I wasn't is likely what has appealed to people, both animal lovers and novice dog owners, who have written to me over the years.

The rescue world is quite different than it was a decade ago. There's more of an effort to find solutions and find homes and to work to prevent pet homelessness rather than scrambling against the clock to place animals after they have become sick, injured, and homeless. Many organizations have found success in the important work of community outreach, providing resources and tools so that pet owners can learn to be better equipped to raise and maintain their animal family members. Social media has played a huge role in creating networks of information sharing and advertising for homeless pets—but it has also inspired a negative, angry breed of "activist" who seems to gain satisfaction not through compassion but through public shaming, name-calling, and in some cases, the outright fabrication of crimes committed by people they've likely never met. In order to be truly effective, our compassion for animals cannot exist in a vacuum that excludes compassion for people, as well. The root cause of many of our pet issues is not "bad people" but rather poverty and poor education that lead to difficult choices for people who have few options available to them.

I still get emails from readers who have just discovered the book and write to me after having just spent a weekend with Brando, Zephyr, and Sula. This is the most difficult part for me, because ten years is a lifetime for dogs, and all three of them are gone. My parents, too, have passed on. I don't ever look back on the pages that tell our story. But it means something enormous to know that in readers' imaginations, they live on.

Ken Foster
February 2016

FOUND

Corner of
Dauphine & Piety

Please contact
(555) 239-0852

how they
find me

DOGS ARE LIKE TATTOOS.

Ask folks about their tattoos and they can tell you exactly what was going on in their lives when they got them, how the idea came to them, why it seemed, at the time, a good thing to do. Even if they had lightning bolts tattooed down their face, to hear them talk about it you realize tattoos are a sentimental art. They mark their owners permanently with a visual memorial of the past. Like dogs do.

I've never had a tattoo, but I've had many dogs, and all of them have left their own indelible marks on me.

• • •

I've found dogs tied under park benches.

Stuck in drainage grates.

Running door to door in the neighborhood with half an eye out.

I've even had a dog delivered to me by police escort when her owners were involved in a domestic dispute.

I've found dogs listed online and placed listings for other dogs to find a home of their own—the dog equivalent of Internet dating.

I've delayed vacations by stopping to pick up a stray dog along the road.

• • •

My friends think I must go looking for them. *Didn't you just find one last week? Do people bring them to your house?*

I tell my friends they don't let themselves see them, because then they would have to do something, too. People ignore stray dogs the same way they ignore stray people, the way your friends in the city insist that they have never seen any homeless people or, when pressed, offer the opinion that these people choose to be on the street and wouldn't want a home if they had one.

I was driving down a Mississippi road with Case, one of my blind-to-dog friends, and spotted a dog on the horizon, wandering down the middle of the road, coming toward us as we sped along in my friend's truck. I let out a sigh.

"What?" Case asked. He may not see dogs, but you can't sigh around him without explaining yourself.

I nodded in the direction of the dog. Case, who was driving, still didn't see anything.

"The dog," I said. We were speeding ever closer, and the dog was still coming toward us. A badly matched game of chicken.

"What dog?"

"Right there!" I yelled, pointing at the windshield.

"Oh him," Case said. "He's always there."

• • •

They find *me*. It isn't ever the other way around. I don't go marching into overgrown patches looking for dogs who don't even know that they are lost. I don't carry a net in my car that I can toss great distances. What happens instead is this: They come up to me and sit at my feet. They tap me with a paw. They loiter in my path waiting for someone to do something. They can't talk. They can't make signs. There is a limit to how much they can tell us.

We are supposedly smarter than they are, but clearly not more intuitive. If we had their skills for assessing a situation I would never see this: car after car swerving to avoid two dachshunds wandering the middle of a highway. Most not even slowing down.

Rescuing something takes time, and there is a risk of revealing something about yourself—your vulnerability—that isn't fashionable at all.

That's what people don't understand. You do it *because* it is difficult. You do it because you aren't sure of things. You do it without knowing how any of it will turn out, or how much it will cost you, or if the story will be happy or tragic in the end.

on being
rescued

IN AUGUST 2001 MY PARENTS DROVE INTO MANHATTAN
to pick up my dog and me for a trip home to Pennsylvania. Earlier that year—momentarily mortified at my decision to get an
animal—they had vowed that my dog Brando and I would
never be allowed in their home, but it was only a few weeks later
that they broke down. This was typical of my parents. They felt
getting a dog was a huge error in judgment, but once it was clear
that my mind was made up on the subject, they wanted to be a
part of the mistake.

Brando was still a puppy, although a huge one. At sixty
pounds he had just begun to lift his leg to pee, and earlier that
day he marked each of the entrances to Tompkins Square, as if
he knew he wouldn't be seeing it for a while. He had traveled
home often enough that he thought any white van was my
parents' white van, and he would sit down on the sidewalk
waiting for a door to open so he could hop inside. He was
stubborn and had otherwise always been reluctant to go anywhere, as if he feared being left behind, but once he had decided to trust people—neighbors, the staff of the hot dog store

down the street—he was obsessive about hunting them down. Sometimes, when he had parked himself on a street corner waiting for someone he had seen there the day before, the only way of getting him to move was to carry him, which I did frequently until he reached fifty pounds. My indulgence only made things worse, although it may have been inevitable that he would develop separation anxiety once I had rescued him—and having rescued him, I was willing to put up with any problem he might have in the future.

On this particular trip my parents were also picking up Laurel—an old friend, my babysitter when I was younger, and the daughter of a neighbor back home in Pennsylvania in our little one-road town. In New York City she lived just two blocks away, closer, perhaps, than she had back home. Brando thought the more people, the better, but still managed to settle into his spot between my parents' bucket seats once the car started moving. We anticipated a long trip, a four-hour drive with plenty of bathroom breaks for the dog. We were trying to decide on the fastest way out of town—south to the tunnel or north to the bridge—when the car died in the middle of Great Jones Street near Lafayette. The drivers behind us responded instantly with honking horns. I ran out to the service station on the corner, where I was told that it would be several days before they could look at it.

It was Laurel's idea to go to the fire station. The men came out of Ladder 9/Engine 33 and helped push the car to the side. They brought out water for Brando while we stood outside in the excruciating summer heat. They walked a block farther to another service station, and the owners agreed to fix the car immediately. Laurel and I joined a couple of the men to help push the car down the street, and Brando helped, too, putting his paws up on the back of the van as we pushed. He had no idea what we were doing, of course. He just wanted to be near me and involved with the other men.

"I've never seen a dog do that before," Laurel said with a laugh.

I, on the other hand, had never seen people in New York as helpful as this fire department. It hadn't even occurred to me that it was a possibility. I loved New York, and particularly my neighborhood, but I still clung to the notion that people were too busy to ask questions of them and that the need for help was an unattractive thing to reveal. This is why I had a dog— Brando never hesitated to make his needs known to me. He was completely unafraid of revealing his vulnerabilities. This is what he taught me.

Of course, there was also the separation anxiety, and for most of the previous eight months I had been struggling with trying to help him, trying to convince him that every time I went out the door there was no question that I would be coming home. By September he was beginning to believe me, but after the World Trade Center came down, even I wasn't so sure. We were in the park when one of the planes flew overhead, and there was a noise that I remember, but don't remember. Although the noise had been deafening, we couldn't see what had happened from the park, and it was hard to believe that it actually was what it had sounded like—a plane flying that low and then crashing.

When something that big happens so close to you, it takes a while before you have any perspective. Brando and I walked home and sat together on the bed, staring at the static on the TV screen where a picture had been before we left. My father called immediately to say he was driving in to get us, and I didn't understand why. Then he called again to tell me that the city had been shut down. My television reception had come from the top of the towers, and after flipping the dial I managed to find one grainy image of the towers in flames. I went outside just in time to see the buildings go down, and even then it took a while for it to really sink in. Later that night I noticed rims of white dust had formed around Brando's nostrils, and I realized that we had all been breathing that in, all day and in the days that followed.

Our neighborhood, below 14th Street, was blocked off from within the city as well. There was no traffic for days, but in the distance there was the constant sound of police and medical sirens. There was no newspaper delivery, no food on store shelves. Even though there were people—and friends—all around us, it seemed as if Brando and I were on our own. For months after, there were mornings when Brando woke up whining in the morning, and I would know that soon I would be able to smell it too—the fires that were still burning downtown. For the following year that I lived in the city, I was reluctant to travel too far from home. I was particularly suspicious of crossing the boundary that had been established at 14th Street. When I did, I experienced a palpable fear that something might happen, and I wouldn't be allowed back home again, and Brando, locked inside the apartment, would never know where I had been all that time or that I hadn't broken the promise I'd made when I rescued him—that I would always return home.

• • •

My parents and I talked a lot by phone during those first days—sometimes calling to let me know what was being reported about things just down the street from where I stood at the time—and my mother said she couldn't stop thinking of the men from the firehouse, and wondering if any of them had been harmed. I didn't want to say anything, because I didn't know for sure, but the general rule of thumb was that the farther downtown a house was, the more men it was likely to have lost. I was on the street with Brando as we spoke, because being on the street in those days after the attacks felt strangely safer than ever: Everyone was out there together, and all the traffic was shut down. Better than staying inside, watching the endless loop of disaster as it replayed on the news.

"We can go over there," I told my mom. "We can bring them something." On the corner there was a deli that had only recently replenished its supply of flowers. I remember the surprise at the end of the week of walking in to get coffee and seeing bread and newspapers on the shelves for the first time in days. It seemed longer.

I picked two clusters of sunflowers. They looked sturdy and huge among the more delicate ones that surrounded them. Brando tried to grab them out of my hand.

"Don't even think about it," I told him. "This is serious." He walked at my side to the station house, where a table was set up outside the doors, overflowing with flowers and notes. I found room in one of the vases to add our sunflowers to the mix and was ready to leave. Brando sat on the sidewalk staring at all the flowers. He didn't want to move. I knelt next to him and put an arm around him. He didn't look at me, just the flowers and tributes that were before us.

Finally I heard a voice say, "Do you want to come in?" I looked up and saw one of the men standing in the open door. I don't think I answered. I don't think I could. He waved us in, and we followed.

There was already a framed tribute set up on an easel inside the door. I looked at the photos of the ten men they had lost, while the fireman fed Brando biscuits. I tried to recognize the men, to figure out if any of them had been the people who had rescued us that day, in our stalled van, on Great Jones Street, but the truth was I hadn't been paying that much attention. Meanwhile, Brando kept asking for another biscuit.

"Sorry," I said, apologizing for Brando, and everything else. "He'll never leave if you keep letting him have those biscuits."

"That's okay," he said. "It's no trouble."

• • •

For months afterward, Brando would lead me back to the firehouse, zigzagging through the streets whenever we got within range. I began trying to lead him around any of the obvious routes there, but he always outsmarted me by making a couple of surprise turns. And, of course, I let him. Brando would sit respectfully in front of the flowers, and the men would call us inside, and Brando would have biscuits, and everything would, strangely, feel normal and right for a few minutes again. I watched other people come by, with flowers and contributions, and I realized how funny it was that we all thought we were coming to check in on them, when the truth was, even then, that the men of the firehouse were inviting us in because they knew it would make us feel better, not them.

• • •

It was sometime after that that I began finding dogs and wanting to rescue them. But each time I do, I find myself having that same puzzling epiphany, wondering if I'm doing it for them or whether in rescuing them, I'm actually doing something for myself.

getting rid of
rocco

ROCCO WAS A CRAZY RED-NOSED PIT BULL WHOM I HAD watched grow from a pup. He didn't even look quite like a dog. His head was huge, his neck nonexistent, and when he ran around the dog run greeting everyone he looked more like a gregarious, rust-colored hog. People were afraid of him, not because of anything he'd done, but because he was a pit bull and pit bulls are supposed to be bad. But Rocco had an owner who watched him like a hawk, calling out his name, stretching the last syllable, anytime it looked like Rocco was bothering someone. When Rocco heard his owner calling he would turn on a dime and head straight back to him, a delirious grin stretching across his crazy dog face.

Rocco and Brando had played together when they were young, racing around the rim of the run. As Rocco grew older, and larger, people would pull me aside when they came in to voice their concern. "That dog shouldn't be in the run."

"Rocco is great," I said.

Rocco was unaltered, which is a sort of status symbol not just with pits, but with purebred dogs of all kinds; the owners feel it is wrong to neuter the dog, even if they have no intention

of breeding him anytime down the line. Intact males are sometimes more aggressive, but often the problem comes from the
neutered males around them, who smell their scent and feel the
need to prove their dominance.

We hadn't seen him for a while when one day he came in
and made his rounds. Rocco leapt up on the picnic table and
licked my face. "Roccooo!" his owner called. "It's okay," I said,
and then I went to get Brando from the other side of the run.
I leashed him up and brought him over to sit with me. Rocco
was wandering alone, and his owner asked why I wasn't letting Brando play with him. "Rocco won't do anything. He's a
good dog."

"It's not Rocco I'm worried about," I confessed. Brando had
been having issues with intact male dogs, sometimes getting
feisty from the smell alone after the dog himself was gone.
There actually seemed to be a number of exceptions Brando was
willing to make for dogs he'd known all his life, but the smell of
intact dogs, new to the run, turned him into a monster. I didn't
want to take a chance with Rocco.

This was around the summer of 2001, and we didn't see
Rocco's owner much afterward. There were a lot of people we
didn't see, and sometimes you had to guess if it was because they
were gone or because they just didn't come out anymore. The
strange part, in the dog run, was that there were people you worried about without ever having known their full names, so there
was no way of checking. Then, eventually, they would show up,
looking just as relieved to see you as you were to see them.

Rocco showed up again, too. On a poster offering him to a
good home. I saw it tacked one day to the bulletin board at the
entrance to the park and read it a few times to make sure it was

him. There was an e-mail address to contact, so I wrote it down and took it home. I didn't know why I had written it down—the last thing I needed was another dog in a studio apartment—but I liked Rocco, and something seemed wrong that his owner, who loved him, too, was putting him in a new home via a flyer in a public park.

Also, New York, like many parts of the country, is notorious for underground dogfighting. There were stories floating around the neighborhood about people stealing dogs who'd been tied up outside the grocery stores to use as bait for training dogs to fight. Putting up an ad offering a purebred pit bull to the first taker was likely to attract the wrong kind of owner—one of the reasons that rescue groups charge a fee is to weed people out during the adoption process. Rocco deserved better than to be given away.

• • •

The week before Thanksgiving I stopped by the dog run and there was Rocco, looking lost. Where before he would prance around the run, drawing an invisible line between his owner and the rest of the people in there, now he was directing all his attention outward, beyond the fence, as if he didn't think he belonged there at all. A woman was screaming at him to come; she had several other pit bulls with her, and when Rocco finally approached her on the bench she punched him in the face. Rocco continued scampering around the run, his head craned as if he was looking for someone. He went to the bathroom and no one picked it up.

"Is that your dog?" someone asked the woman whom I had seen hit him.

"No," she said. Yet a few minutes later she was calling for him to come again. She gathered up all her dogs and jumped over the fence. The dogs followed her, but not Rocco, so she pulled him over the fence by his leash. He toppled over the fencetop and fell to the ground.

Everyone in the run was talking now. No one had ever seen the woman before. No one wanted her back.

"I know that dog," I said. "He doesn't belong to her." I had the dizzy feeling you get when you're watching an accident approach in slow motion.

I went home and e-mailed his owner, describing what I'd seen. I added:

I know you are looking for a good home for him, and he is a great dog. This girl is the last person that should spend any time with him. I wish I could take him, but I can't for a number of reasons. But if you can't keep him and can't find a home for him other than with this rotten person, let me know. If nothing else, I know of a lot of good, responsible, private, no-kill dog shelters; of course, they would want to neuter him, but I'd rather see that than see him turned nasty from abuse.

The response was quick:

Thanks Ken.
I will deal with her as soon as I can find her. I've been calling her home phone since I gave her the

dog last Saturday (11/17), and I've been getting no response. I'm not even sure if the person you saw Rocco with is the same person. Could you please describe her to me? I would also like to get some info on those no-kill shelters you talked about.

The only reason I gave her Rocco was because she seemed very sincere and I've actually known her for quite some time.

Please call me @ home 212-674-XXXX or I'll call you.

I'm going to try to get Rocco back and give him to a no-kill.

I tried my best to type out a description, but I had been paying more attention to Rocco than to the woman who was abusing him. She had long dark hair. She was wearing leather. That could describe anyone in our neighborhood. "I didn't think you would have left him with someone that was going to treat him like that," I wrote, "though I did worry for a minute after I sent the e-mail that you might say something like 'Hey, that's my sister.' There were actually other people in the run who commented on the way she was acting, even though they didn't know Rocco or the situation with him, so it was pretty obviously out-of-place dog owner behavior. And I've never seen you treat the dog that way . . ." I wanted him to know that my concern was for the dog, not anything he might have done.

• • •

The owner responded, and explained why he had gotten rid of Rocco. It was because of 9/11:

> Thanks a lot Ken.
>
> I don't think you have any idea how I'm feeling right now. But just to sum up . . . I feel like I betrayed him and I feel like wringing that bitch's neck! I had to give him up even though I didn't want to. Due to the tragedy, I've been forced to work long hours @ my job. He was being neglected. I couldn't get home and walk him on time. His nails were getting overgrown, he was losing weight, and he was generally just miserable. I thought me giving him up was the best way for his sake . . .

I e-mailed him info on shelters that might be able to help. I put the word out around the run. The whole thing made me sick, though, because Rocco was such a terrific dog, but his breed attracted the wrong person. Pit bulls are stolen from yards constantly, used for fighting, or bred to sell by people whose only interest is in making some easy money. At some point, in my frustration, I used the phrase "if I'd known you were going to throw him away." I probably even claimed that I would have taken him in—an absurd claim given my closet-sized apartment. The response:

> . . . just for the record I didn't think that I was throwing him away. The girl seemed very nice, and I've seen her with her dogs for quite some time. She and her mother have had a male pit for many years already. I let her get acquainted with Rocco before I gave her to him, and in front of me she

treated him very well. He also took to her very well. When I find her she is going to get interrogated!!!

After that flurry of e-mail, I didn't hear any more, and I didn't see the woman or Rocco again. Then, on Christmas Eve, I was at my sister's house in Michigan when I got another e-mail. This one was grim:

Bad news about Rocco. The girl I gave him to lost him!!! He was last seen running up Avenue D about a week ago!

My heart is broken.

If you hear absolutely anything please let me know.

If I were to find him again I'd keep him and just try to make the best of it.

I didn't believe the story at all. A runaway dog on Avenue D? And no one has seen him? More likely, she decided to sell him for some cash the week before Christmas, and in my e-mail back to him, I suggested my suspicion.

Ken

I seriously feel like beating the shit out of her. I told her not to let him loose and she didn't listen. A couple people told me the facts before she sugared up her story. They (the people) told me that she let him loose to make him walk by her side right on Ave. D (the xxxxxg dumb xxxx!!!), and he saw his chance and just took off like greased lightning and she never saw him again. I used to walk him all over the place, and he knew the area pretty well. I only hope he didn't try to go to the East River Park because he would have gotten run over by a car. :(

Perhaps he tried to go to the run . . .

No one ever saw Rocco again.

I thought about what might have happened if I had been quicker. If I had said something as soon as I saw that sign. If I had done something when I saw that lousy woman punch the dog in the face. So now, whenever I see a pit bull wandering along a road, I always pull my car over and invite him in.

how to
lose your
best friend

———

1. Invite him to live with you, but only if he stays outside.

2. Tie a rope around his neck so he knows where he belongs.

3. Insist on feeding him, but only the cheapest things available.

4. Make him accompany you on your errands, and while you are shopping, make him wait outside.

5. When you go on vacation for a week, leave a little something extra in his bowl.

6. Tell yourself, *They survive on their own in the wild*, even though your yard is not the wild, and in the wild they only live a short time.

7. After a few years, consider abandoning him, because it isn't fun anymore and you are bored. Consider the same about your spouse, your friends, and your children, too.

8. You're too busy to train him, but it's his fault if he doesn't know commands.

9. When people ask, explain that leash laws are for the other dogs.

10. Assume, despite all evidence to the contrary, that he'll be fine without you, that someone else will step in to take your place, that after all this time, he won't even know that you are gone.

abandoning
sinatra

EVEN IF YOU LOVE DOGS, IT'S NOT HARD TO IMAGINE THE reasons why someone would choose to abandon one. Dogs are demanding. Dogs have expectations for us to fulfill. What's bewildering is that some people actually follow through with the impulse to drop their pet out the door of their car, or tie him to a street lamp, or set him free in the woods thinking that he can fend for himself on his own. For those of us who raise dogs, the challenges are part of the appeal. And perhaps that's the key difference between dogs and other domestic pets: We *raise* them. It's rare to hear that term used in connection with any other animal in a home: People don't talk about raising tropical fish or birds or guinea pigs. Even cats are more often *had* than raised. But dogs grow up with us.

I get cornered all the time by people who are considering getting a dog and want to know what to expect. "If I get an older dog," they ask, "will I have to train him?" Yes, I tell them, even though there are plenty of older dogs who have certainly grown out of their rambunctious puppyhood. Part of it, I said, is about establishing a relationship, so that even if they know the commands, they will need to know what they mean coming from you, the new owner. "You can't just install them in the apartment like a piece of furniture," I say, and these people usually say something along the lines of "Oh, never mind." These are not dog people, and that is fine, as long as they don't have dogs. The dog person, hearing how difficult and challenging it may be to take a rescued dog from a shelter, signs up for the responsibility immediately, ready to cancel vacations and sacrifice the new couch.

Like parents who abandon their children at day care or leave the newborn child on the steps of a hospital or a church, many people who decide to get rid of a dog take him somewhere they think they'll find someone better able to take care of him: a vet's office, a park, a dog run. Then they leave him behind, pretending, I guess, that they've done everything they can.

• • •

When Brando was younger we would sometimes spend hours in the dog run in Tompkins Square, and during the time we were there entire populations of dogs would come and go while we sat and talked and played. Sometimes, on weekends, there were so many dogs it was difficult to know whom they belonged to. One afternoon I noticed a small collie huddled under the bench and didn't think anything of it, because I was used to strange dogs coming and sitting right next to me. Once, a rottweiler named Madonna came and sat with me, resting her head on my shoulder. A man at the next bench asked, "That's not your dog, is it?" astonished that I would allow the animal to be so familiar with me.

On this day, after a couple of hours of getting up and down and wandering the grounds, I realized the collie was still there. When a group of dogs were playing chase and tried to squeeze behind the bench, a small fight broke out. Everyone came running to see if their own dog was involved, but no one came to check the little collie, who was still shaking underneath the bench.

"I don't think that dog belongs to anyone," I said as the crowd cleared. One of my friends began shouting, "Whose dog is this?" No one came. Then we saw why the dog hadn't tried moving: Someone had tied him to the bench with string. We coaxed him out and instantly noticed his bright blue eyes as he looked up at us. He was trembling.

• • •

This is the first case I can remember, but it wasn't unusual, particularly on weekends, for dogs to materialize tied to the fence of the dog run, usually small dogs, lapdogs, the kind of dogs you wouldn't imagine anyone needing to get rid of in such a hurry. The trick was for them to leave the dog there at a time it was so busy no one would notice, or early in the morning, before anyone was there at all. The response of those of us who lived (it seemed) in the run was complex. Rage at the person who left the dog, not just for the act itself, but also for the assumption that we would take care of things. And yet we always did. A crowd inevitably circled the dog, and people would voice options: who could foster the dog, who knew someone who was looking to adopt a dog, who was willing, but only if it was absolutely necessary, to take the dog for a night. I lived in a studio apartment that was barely large enough for my futon, and Brando, who was quickly revealing himself to be part Dane. I was good at recruiting volunteers, but I wasn't really one myself just yet.

"My bartender said he wanted to get a dog," someone said. It sounded like a long shot to me.

"No, really. He's a great guy," she said.

Another person offered to take him home. I left with Brando, but I kept thinking about the dog under the bench and where he would find a home. There's a strange intimacy between a lost animal and the person who finds him. In terms of time, what you've shared is tiny and insignificant, but that moment is a vital pivot in the animal's life, the line between his old life and a better, new one. In some cases that fine line is the one between life and death. It's easy to get cheesy and sentimental about it, and the truth is that what transpires in that moment of finding a lost dog is really not that compelling. The person who saves a dog is not saving the world—so it is remarkable that more people don't make the effort. But the people with the longest list of reasons why they can't help—they are too busy, there are too many other causes that are more important than some animal—aren't really likely to appear on the volunteer lists of any charitable organization. It's not just the dogs they are too busy for.

If you take the time to pull over, to call for help, or to even just deliver the dog to the nearest shelter and check in on him now and then, you will not find yourself subsequently jobless, homeless, or confined to a life alone.

The dogs always remember.

Their new people do, too. I don't know who found Brando on the streets of Brooklyn at Christmastime in 2000, but I often think of that invisible person, and wonder what made them stop, and take that little dog in, and think to drop him off at a shelter as wonderful and dedicated as BARC, where I ultimately met him. I think of that person as often as I think of the other one, who left him on the street. But if I'm going to be honest about it, I have to also confess that before Brando, I walked by stray dogs and put them out of my mind. One in particular haunts me: a bichon frise scrounging for food in the gutter of Avenue B. What made me keep walking? Fear, I suppose. Not of the dog, but of responsibility. Fear of feeling something. Fear of recognizing that dog's vulnerability and my own.

• • •

One of the great perversions of owning a dog in the city is that you begin recognizing dogs instead of the people with them. The people are accessories. I had heard that the dog had found a home—with the bartender, who had named him Sinatra because of his blue eyes. The strange thing is that I'd encountered them on the street a few times before putting them together. Sinatra was a new dog now: cleaned up, proud. There are few things as amusing as a dog who likes showing off his owner, and that is what I noticed first about the two of them in the park; everything the dog did pointed attention toward the man he was with.

"I was the one who found him that day," I said finally one day. "Well, there was a group of us," I added, because it seemed wrong to take any credit for having done so little.

"Really?" he said. It was like I was a celebrity, which is exactly how I would feel if I met any of the people who had found my own dogs. One morning when Brando and I were playing in the park, a young woman stopped and asked, "Is *that* Brando?" For a moment I experienced a surge of social anxiety, trying to place this woman who seemed to be a total stranger.

"I used to walk him," she said. "When he was still at BARC. I never imagined he would get so big."

"Neither did I," I said. "Did he actually walk with you?" I was thinking of the way he never wanted to go anywhere when he was younger, stubbornly planting his ass on the ground and refusing to budge.

"Not really," she said. A wave of relief passed over me, knowing now that it wasn't just me.

What would the human equivalent be? Meeting someone's old college roommate? Their school bus driver? The substitute teacher who somehow made a difference? I don't really know.

• • •

A year later Brando and I were out along the river and I saw the bartender and his dog jogging together. As they approached I said, "Hey, that's Sinatra, isn't it?" Neither of them seemed to remember me, which was fine. "I was one of the people who found him," I reminded him, feeling again that I was exaggerating my role a bit, but wanting to assure him that I wasn't some kind of stalker. He suddenly softened. "He's changed my life," he said. "I mean it. He really changed my life." I looked down at the blue eyes staring up at him as he spoke. "Thank you," the man said. "Thank you for finding him."

As we were leaving he added, "His name is Frankie now. I mean, look at him; I couldn't saddle him with that his whole life."

how dogs
correct us

I CALL BRANDO MY FIRST DOG, ALTHOUGH IT ISN'T REALLY TRUE. We had a family dog when I was too young to know much of anything, a Samoyed named Samantha who traveled home with us as a puppy, perfectly snuggled between my older brother's and sister's legs on the station wagon seat. In winter we would try to get her to pull us through the snow on a sled, and within a few feet she would hear our laughter and run back to join us on the toboggan seat. We fed her table scraps and hideous dog "hamburgers" that seemed made from plastic, colored bright red. Occasionally, she would run away, and the neighbors would call us to let us know where she was. But she wasn't mine. She just was.

Later, when I was living in Oregon, my friend Scholle had a dog named Ellie who went with her everywhere, and when she couldn't come along, Scholle lamented Ellie's absence and felt guilty about her limitations as a dog's friend. This struck me as foreign, too. I just didn't get it, and later, when I lived in New York City, I would watch people with their dogs, in the park, on the street, and I would feel . . . nothing. I wasn't against dogs, but their presence in the world puzzled me, particularly the role they seemed to play among the humans who had taken them in.

When I arrived in Costa Rica in fall 2000, I was planning to spend the three months there working on a new book. I wasn't sure at the time exactly what it would be. My hosts arrived at the airport and drove me silently through the rainy unpaved mountain roads to the small apartment on the farm were I would be living. As one of the hosts finished showing me around in the dark, a small, wet dog emerged from a grove of trees, his stub of a tail wagging in the light of the moon.

"That's Duque," he said.

Duque was a smart dog, and he was smart all on his own. He would follow me home from lunch to take a nap beneath my desk, and after about forty minutes he was gone again, out to follow the gardener on his afternoon rounds. It didn't take long for me to realize Duque was right. Afternoon naps were good. Then he began appearing for dinner, and at night he would sleep on the chair at the foot of my bed, facing the door. He never slept in the bed, even when I invited him. He didn't think it was his place, and seemed offended at the suggestion.

During the times we spent together, he led me around the property, pausing over the most exquisite views, racing with me through the orchards, showing me how much fun it can be to watch a squirrel run up and down a tree. These were things I had forgotten about, even though they surrounded me every day, even in the city.

Duque was always happy to see me. He felt the need to check in on all his friends. If he wanted something he wasn't afraid to ask for it. He had expectations of people, but was forgiving when they let him down. He was the opposite of me, and I wanted to bring him home. When that wasn't allowed, I bought as much dog food as I could get my hands on to leave with one of the housekeepers, along with the dog. I knew the food would run out. I knew that he would end up surviving on scraps of whatever they could give him. But I also hoped that by doing this they would understand how valuable he was—even with so many other stray dogs around.

After returning to New York, I found myself unable to do anything. Duque had set my schedule so efficiently, leaving me to work in the morning, returning to check on my progress at lunch, putting me to bed early in the evening so that my brain could rest and begin the day again. Dogs like a schedule. They like routine. But they also like variety. People tend to go toward one extreme.

If I was going to get anything done, I would need a dog to work with me as a pacer.

Dogs rely on their instincts, and almost everything they do makes perfect, logical sense. If only we could say the same of ourselves. Even dogs with fears follow a logical pattern. Dogs are suspicious of strangers. Dogs don't trust liars or people with sticks. Dogs believe in hard work, and after hard work they believe it is time to rest. Dogs resist separation, and at the same time limit their own pack to a manageable size. Dogs give a warning before they attack.

Meanwhile, we try as much as possible to hide our true feelings, challenge our fears, and diffuse our energy by exploring every possible option.

Dogs are so much more efficient.

the four-hour
custody
limit

WHEN BRANDO AND I STOPPED GOING TO THE DOG RUN, WE
spent most of our time along the river, where there were large
caged-in playing fields where people ran their dogs in the
morning. At first we seemed to be the only people there, but
more and more dog owners were showing up, tossing balls
for their own dogs. It was particularly populated with dogs
like Brando, who had issues of one kind or another, but who
seemed to relax a bit more in the unlimited space along the
East River. Sometimes we would walk farther down to the
Brooklyn Bridge, where there was a wonderful little dog run
that had banned unaltered males and never seemed to have
more than three dogs at a time. Brando loved it there, but he
loved it so much that it was sometimes impossible to get him to
take the long walk back home once we were done. One day, as
we crossed through Chinatown, we passed the local residents
lined along the river going through their morning tai chi routine. Brando dropped the blue ball he was carrying and watched
the ball roll over the edge into the river. He sat staring at the
water, waiting for the ball to resurface. He didn't want to go

home without it. Finally I coaxed him back to our own neighborhood, and we went to the pet store on 14th Street, where, miraculously, we found a ball just like the one he had lost. Now I had to worry that this might become the routine: dropping the ball in the river and racing to the pet store, where it would magically appear, sealed in plastic, on the shelf.

Brando was already obsessed with the pet store, particularly the rabbits that were caged on the floor in the back. Every time we went there, Brando would lie in front of the cages, sometimes pressing his nose against their bars. Sometimes the rabbits pressed their noses back.

Along the river, just at the end of our block, there was a small playground that was understandably empty at six in the morning, so we could close ourselves in securely and play fetch until other dogs came along. More often we took a corner of a ball field that had large open spots along the fence; I had to position Brando in the batting corner when I pitched to him, so that he'd have to run past me to escape. If he did escape, it was likely to find Angus, the black Lab who lived down the street and played fetch with his two mommies at another part of the river. Brando was obsessed with the three of them, and jealous, I imagined, that Angus got to live with two people instead of just one. The more he didn't get to see them, the more excited he became when he did, stealing Angus's ball and refusing to let go of it, delighted to be the center of attention. My goal on these mornings was always to exhaust him as much as possible before people started showing up with their dogs.

I loved those mornings, getting up sometimes before the light had come, walking the streets of the city with everything quiet, still, and orderly. For an hour, it was all ours, with just a few remnants remaining from the day before to suggest that there were others lurking in the landscape.

One morning as I tossed Brando's ball, I had the sense of being watched. I looked up to see a small mutt watching us from outside the fence. She seemed to be waiting for an invitation to join in the fun, but stood very shyly, not coming too close and not trying to run. Brando and I walked out from the softball field, and the puppy came toward us, awkward and tentative, waiting for some direction. She was mostly white, with a few patches of color, as if she might have been part beagle and maybe part pit. There was a collar and, more bewildering, a tattered leash that she had been dragging along behind her, but she was sopping wet. It had rained during the night.

Soon enough another of our friends came by with her dog. She slowed as she realized there was an extra dog with us. "Who is that?" she asked.

"I don't know."

We had a little conference about what to do. Our friend had an office job, which excused her from doing much more than expressing her concern about the dog and her admiration for my doing the right thing. Of course, her admiration for my "doing the right thing" meant I was going to have to do the right thing. I had the time, theoretically. I was still managing to squeak by on freelance work, so I didn't have to be anywhere that morning. On the other hand, that didn't mean I had the time or room for another dog in my life, even temporarily. I hadn't really decided what "the right thing" was at this point. One thing I knew: I didn't want to take the dog home.

Walking with Brando and the mystery dog, one leash in each hand, I came across a group of squatters spread out in sleeping bags under the 10th Street pedestrian bridge. The puppy ran all around the sleeping heads as if she belonged there.

"Is this your dog?" I asked loudly.

No response.

"Excuse me," I shouted.

There was movement. The puppy continued to try to revive the bodies as well, taking a step or two in between them, as if she was ready to nestle there among them. She wasn't timid around them at all, but I wasn't sure if she knew them or just realized that a sleeping body posed no threat.

Finally I was screaming at them, because it seemed to me that either they were now pretending to be asleep or they were close to dead. Still no response. I gave up. At this point, even if they were the owners of the dog, they had failed the test required to get her back.

"Let's go," I said, and the three of us walked toward home, past home, and kept walking until we reached the vet. The doctor wasn't yet in, but Susanne, the receptionist/Brando's crush, looked the dog over and pressed her distended belly.

"She definitely has worms," she said. I had been hoping the vet would just take her off my hands, but that wasn't going to happen. I'd have to pay for a complete checkup before they could board her, and I didn't want to do that if there was a chance she belonged to someone else, or someone else might give in and take over the responsibility. We walked back to the apartment, where I placed her in Brando's crate and let him sit with me on the bed. I slid food and water into the crate, and the puppy devoured both. I gave her more water and she finished the bowl. It seemed she hadn't had anything to drink in a while, despite the fact that she was wet.

Brando got off the bed and lay next to the crate, making google eyes at her. She edged toward him. He was a lonely dog in those days. Our building had recently become infested with mice, and I had decided that glue traps were preferable to snapping traps. But now at night I would wake up and find Brando curled up with glued-down rodents that he had collected around him, where he would lick and groom them as if they were his own. I imagined the mice would prefer a quick death to that torture.

As I watched Brando get comfortable with his new mate, I sent out e-mails to everyone I knew. "She and my dog are getting along too well," I wrote before asking that anyone who might help contact me immediately. I looked at the clock. It was just past ten. I decided that she needed to be gone by two at the latest.

I called all the shelters I could find. None of them was even open yet. Finally I got hold of Robert at Social Tees, a T-shirt shop that also did animal rescue. He wasn't sure he could find a place for her, but said that if I came by later in the afternoon he would take a look. A student e-mailed me from her job at Cooper Union saying her boss might be interested, and I suggested I walk the dog over and meet them around lunch. Meanwhile my friend Amanda Davis had forwarded the e-mail already to her enormous list of friends. This was typical Amanda, although technically she was a cat person. Earlier in the year, when some friends had a spare Rhodesian ridgeback, it had been Amanda who set up the dog with his soul mate, a woman who spent her weekends hiking with him in the country. Soon enough I had an e-mail from Amanda's friend Kate, who admitted, "I've already squandered at least 200 hours on Petfinder.com looking at puppy porn! Sadly we keep finding perfect mutts in Virginia. I know, I know, must set geographical limit on browser." Despite all these leads, I was in a panic that if I didn't get her out of my house soon, she would never leave. Brando, or me, or both of us, would have trouble giving her up.

We left the house again and walked over to meet the women from Cooper Union. They bent down and greeted the puppy, considered her, but they needed time. Brando kept wedging his way between the ladies and the other dog, and I wasn't sure if he was jealous or protective. From there we walked back to Social Tees on 4th Street, but no one was there. I decided I'd rather wait on the street than have to go back to the apartment with two dogs. Brando settled next to her on the sidewalk, and I watched as they slowly inched their front paws toward each other until, eventually, they were facing each other with their paws intertwined.

When Robert, the owner, finally arrived, he took one look at the dogs and said, "I'll take her," before he'd even finished unlocking the door.

"I thought you weren't sure," I said.

"I didn't realize how big your other dog was," he explained. I wasn't sure if he was concerned about the lack of space in my apartment or the possibility that Brando would swallow her whole. Inside the shop were aquariums of reptiles, his specialty, which he rehabilitated from living neglected in apartments and then placed in classrooms where they could be cared for and used as educational tools to instruct kids in biology and responsibility. He also had a cageful of rescued ferrets nestled in a suspended nest and photographs of previous rescues, including one snapshot of a bulldog posing with a capuchin monkey.

When Brando and I returned to the apartment, it seemed awfully quiet and dull. I sat alone on the bed; Brando stared at his now empty crate. Neither of us could get back to our usual work: my writing, Brando's soap operas.

I called Robert the next day, and he told me that the dog had gone to a family the previous afternoon. They had been looking for a second dog and were thrilled to find her.

Most rescue stories end there. You try not to think about the animals. You can't really allow it. The one thing you can generally be sure of is that they are certain to be better off than when you found them. In this case I had done such a good job of getting the word out that I kept hearing back from people. First, Amanda's friend Kate, who had just come back to town and was ready to finally meet the dog, but had missed her chance on this one. Then, more unexpectedly, this one:

Dear Ken:

Hi . . . My name is Lisa. I e-mailed you last week after you found the puppy at the East River Park. Well, I found the owner of the puppy. She is a 23-year-old girl named Shayla. She lost the puppy in the East River Park. The puppy had tags on her but apparently they had fallen off between the time she lost her dog and when you found her. Robert, at Social Tees, has already found a family for the dog. I have not spoken to Shayla, but her social worker has been in touch with me through a youth center that she belongs to and apparently the girl is very distraught. They are trying to get the dog through Social Tees, but Robert is not being too helpful. He says he cannot get in touch with the family who has the dog and is questioning why the dog did not have tags on it. Many times when a dog is lost it can lose its tags. Who knows what happens . . . The social worker would like to try to get in touch with the new owners directly, but Robert will not give out their info . . . There is a flyer up at the Tompkins Sq dog run with a pic of the dog and all the info about the lost dog—this is how I found the owner of the lost dog. Do you have any suggestions how I can help this girl be reunited with her dog before another day goes by? Robert actually told the social worker that the puppy is so sweet that he hates to take it from the new family . . . I know if my dog was missing, I wouldn't sleep, eat etc. until he was home safe!!!

My cell phone # is 917-549-XXXX if you can think of anything!!
thanks!!!
lisa

Apparently, I had given away someone else's dog. I was in the middle of a custody dispute. A small part of me felt awful, but a larger part was baffled at the details of the situation. When I had found the dog, she had a torn leash but no tags. I found it difficult to understand the law of physics that would allow the tags to be separated from the dog, but not the leash or collar. More than that, what was a social worker doing advocating for the return of a dog? For a twenty-three-year-old mother who, judging from her involvement in a youth center, was likely single, and judging from the condition of the dog, unable to juggle her own life with that of a child *and* a dog.

Luckily, I was actually in no position to reveal anything—I had no idea where the dog was, either. I e-mailed Lisa and explained all of this, as well as the rather bad condition the dog seemed to be in when I found her—something that would have required more than a night alone in the park to develop. As a side note, I wondered how a social worker in New York City even had the time to be bothered with something like this. Lisa wrote back:

> Well, I was confused when this girl's social worker called me so I don't really understand what is going on to be honest. All I know is that the girl is 23 and was in the park with the dog and her kid and the kid had the dog and somehow the kid lost the dog. The girl belongs to Safe Horizon which is some kind of youth center . . . It took me three calls to this place since Sat to get a call back today . . . Now I'm confused too . . . It seems to me like the girl most likely doesn't know how to take care of a dog and most likely herself as well . . .
>
> You are probably right . . . ughhh!!!!
> thanks for getting back to me!!!!—Lisa

For weeks I kept waiting for more phone calls, more intrigue, an unexpected confrontation of some kind. But nothing came. Eventually Brando and I stopped looking for the little dog in the margins of our game playing along the river each morning. She was gone to us. She had moved on into a kind of anonymous witness protection program, and all we could do, when her memory floated into our consciousness, was remind ourselves that she was better off now, she was being taken care of. She was part of a family, somewhere, off beyond the distance.

how to
read a dog

Posture is everything. Rigid and domineering means exactly that. The vast majority of dogs—even the most aggressive of them—prefer to give clear warnings before taking action. If the hair rises on their backs and their posture becomes more erect, they're letting you know that they feel threatened and are ready to defend themselves. On the other hand, if they tumble onto their backs and roll around at your feet, you have nothing to fear.

Trust your instincts. More than that, if a dog's behavior makes you uncomfortable, your fear will further raise the dog's suspicions. The more fearful you are, the more likely the dog is to be aggressive.

Every dog has its own individual expressions. It is important to learn the idiosyncrasies of your own animal's gestures. For example, Brando has a particular growl that actually means: *I need a peanut butter biscuit*. He has a way of scratching his chest that means he's feeling shy around new people.

Learn to understand and anticipate the generalizations dogs make in our world. Dogs can respond with fear and aggression to things they simply don't understand. If you are working with stray animals, it's important to realize—or anticipate—the possibility that their response in any given moment might be inspired by a stick or a hat or a sound that their brain has wired as something worthy of suspicion. Similarly, dogs can't be expected to understand that Brando's peanut butter biscuit growl isn't directed at them or that a husky bred to have a dominant posture might not have the personality to match.

Learn the difference between play and aggression. Two dogs who are truly playing with each other will follow certain rules. Upon meeting each other, they face off and bow—a mix of aggression (the approach) and submission (bowing to a more vulnerable level below the other dog's mouth). The rest of the play will become a combination of these moves, with the two dogs taking turns chasing and being chased, trying out new moves on each other to test one another out. A playfully aggressive move is generally followed by a bow or a posture that invites the other dog to take charge. But sometimes this balance falls out of whack. One dog begins to push too much, taking on only the aggressive role, refusing to back down. As with children, when it is no longer fun for everyone involved, it is time to stop.

two halves
of a bone

SOME PEOPLE LEAVE THEIR ANIMALS BEHIND. MAYBE THEIR new home doesn't allow pets. Maybe their new spouse doesn't like the dog. Or possibly, absurdly, they figure that abandoning the animal is easier than moving him along with everything else in the van. People get rid of dogs around the holidays for the same reason. I once heard of an award-winning novelist who had his dogs euthanized every time he needed to move—it was easier to just get a set of new ones once the house was settled.

The point of living with dogs is not that they are there to make our lives easier. The point, I think, is that they are primarily a responsibility, and yet in being responsible for them, we get a lot back. They reward us.

The summer we started finding dogs was also the summer we had planned to move. Well, I had planned to move. Brando knew nothing about it. I had been thinking of moving ever since I'd returned from Costa Rica. I had been planning to move when I got Brando as a pup. But after that September, I'd stayed in New York, partly volunteering at the Here Is New York photography project, and partly because I didn't want to be among the people who appeared to give up.

Now, after too much volunteering and not enough freelance income, I was in debt.

"You can't afford that dog," my mother said.

"I can afford the dog," I insisted. "It's just everything else that's pushing me into debt."

The city was having money problems, too, and one of its solutions was to begin enforcing the dog regulations. No more playing fetch in Tompkins Square, and eventually they began patrolling our secret ball-playing court along the river. One morning, while homeless people lay passed out around us and one woman was going to the toilet behind a tree, an officer fined me $250 for playing with Brando inside the abandoned playground. I tried to argue that playing with him in the isolation of those gates was the responsible thing to do, but the officer wasn't listening. He also wasn't at all concerned with the human defecation going on while we spoke. Enraged, I sent announcements to the local press stating my plans to leave town in response to the mayor's outrageous crackdown on responsible dog owners. It was totally over the top, but it felt good when I was done. I had forgotten about it completely when a friend called the following week to tell me I was featured in the *New York Post*'s notorious "Page Six" gossip column.

I took a job in Tallahassee, teaching at Florida State. As our move approached, Brando became more nervous, and his nervousness was expressed in aggression. I have no doubt he was picking up on my own anxiety—I wasn't ready to move, and I resented the people in the neighborhood who were settled comfortably into spacious apartments that I could never dream of having. Brando growled at them on the street. He growled at the ridgebacks whom he had once happily trailed behind in the park. Our own apartment was being slowly emptied as I whittled down my possessions for the move. Brando didn't like this. His previous owner had probably walked him through all of these steps before abandoning him—that was as much as I knew of his story, pieced together by the shelter staff by tracing his rabies tag to the original vet.

Our walks became more important. One day, walking along the river to Fishbridge Park, I decided on a detour across the Williamsburg Bridge into Brooklyn. It's a huge bridge, with a walkway and a metal grid floor that you can look through, but Brando wasn't bothered by any of this, even though he's a dog who stammers in terror at the appearance of a drainage grate on the street. By the time we reached the midpoint Brando had taken the lead, enthusiastically tugging at the leash and turning to make sure I was keeping up with him. When we reached Brooklyn he turned right, then left, and then walked for a block before stopping at the front door of an old loft building.

A year earlier, when I had been with Brando for just six months, he had lived in this building for ten days while I taught in a summer program in Iowa. His dogsitter had been Susanne, the receptionist from the vet's office. Brando loved Susanne so much that when we met in Tompkins Square for her to pick him up, he walked off with her without looking back at me. I was flabbergasted, but at least I didn't need to worry about him while I was teaching. Meanwhile, he drove Susanne and her boyfriend crazy, worming his way into their bedroom at night. It was his first and last vacation at their house; a few months later when I needed to go away again, Susanne passed on the opportunity.

But Brando still remembered.

"They don't live there anymore," I told him as he stood in front of the door, waiting for someone to open it. I coaxed him away from the door, and we walked north until he stopped me again, at BQE, the pet store run by BARC where eighteen months earlier I had paid my adoption fee before taking him home. As far as I knew, he had never been there before, and it was too early on a Sunday morning for anyone else to be there, so we stood outside the closed shop for a few minutes before continuing up the street. I wanted to see if he would find one more place that even I didn't know the address to.

Ten minutes later we were outside the door of the warehouse that had served as a temporary kennel during the time Brando was a BARC orphan. It was behind this door that I had first met Brando, where he would tumble out of his cage each time I visited and collapse at my feet, where every time I took him for a walk he was afraid to travel any farther than the spot where we were now standing.

We went to get breakfast at a café down the street, and on the way back to the bridge we stopped at the BQE again. There was a side door open, and some dogs were being walked now. Brando sat and watched until one of the men came to us.

"This is Brando," I said. "He came from here."

"You want to give him back?" the man asked.

"No!" I said. "We're moving to Florida. We just came across the bridge today for a walk and he found his way back here."

"Hold on," the man said, and he disappeared into the store, returning with a bagful of biscuits and pig ears. "A going-away present."

• • •

On moving day my parents arrived in the van, and Brando prepared himself for a vacation. He was surprised when the car kept going, past my parents' house in Pennsylvania, all the way south to Florida. We slept in motel rooms along the way, my parents in one bed, Brando and I in the other. Once I was asleep, Brando would leap from my bed onto my parents', where he would squeeze his way in between their bodies and then stretch out, taking more and more space as the night passed.

Once, I looked over in the middle of the night to see his silhouette rising up like the Great Pumpkin between their sleeping bodies, and then sinking down again. I decided to rescue my parents by coaxing him back to my side of the room. He wasn't budging. I grabbed his collar; he assumed a slack civil-disobedience posture that made it impossible to move him. By now my mother was awake, and she got out of bed to help me as we each took an end and tried to carry Brando away. His ninety-pound body sagged between us like a giant wet noodle. We were doubled over laughing but we wouldn't give up. My father still had his eyes shut, but had to be faking. Finally we got the dog back into my bed.

The next morning at breakfast my mother and I exchanged a silent glance when Dad said, "At least Brando didn't try to sleep with us last night."

• • •

In Tallahassee we lived in the Shoney's Inn for a week while I looked at rental houses before settling on the first one I had seen. There Brando had stubbornly parked his body on the lawn, refusing to get back in the car. I'd kept looking, but it turned out Brando was right. It was a ranch house, with more rooms than I could use, but it also had a fenced backyard so we would be able to play without worrying about bothering anyone else. There were banana and plum and pecan trees, and a little forest of bamboo along the back fence. What I didn't realize was how different it would be having our own space. In the city you have to get up in the middle of the night sometimes so the dog can go outside, and Brando would stare at me impatiently wondering why I was bothering to get dressed when all we were doing was going to the bathroom. Here, all I needed to do was open the door and send him out—but I hadn't realized how much you know and understand about your dog's health by the close monitoring of that daily routine. When a city dog is sick, you know it immediately. With suburban dogs, you don't catch things quite so quickly.

The house was at an intersection, and there were dogs in fenced yards at each corner. Brando kept an eye on them from the bay window, waiting to see who owned them. We were out for a walk when he first spotted Lisa, who lived directly across from Brando's window; for days he had been watching her dog, Bumpy, play in the yard. Brando broke free of my grip and raced across the lawn to her, collapsing at her feet. He also rolled over on his back at the other corner, in front of a fourteen-year-old golden retriever named Dusty. These were his new, immediate friends. At the remaining house, a group of college students shared a rottweiler and two pit bulls who didn't seem to have any names.

Visiting neighbors wasn't enough for a dog used to life in the city, so I began taking Brando out while I rode on my bicycle. Initially I just wanted to show him what the bike was, because whenever I rolled it out he was terrified. Soon he was running alongside me while I held the leash and handlebar in one hand. Then he started to outpace me. He pulled me at high speed through the neighborhood, glancing over his shoulder at me now and then to see if I was still there, like the Grinch's dog pulling his sled. This was our routine. Until a squirrel came along. Brando followed. I slammed on the brakes and flew through the air and landed on my shoulder in the middle of the street.

It wasn't until the swelling went down later in the week that I realized what had happened: My right clavicle was snapped in two. You hear people talk about extreme pain, you think you know what they mean . . . and then you actually experience it. I couldn't do anything. There was no way of setting the bone, and I didn't have insurance, so the specialist who "treated" me told me to just take it easy for a few months and avoid anything that might interfere with the healing. I had seen the X-rays—the two halves were barely touching. Throughout the day I could feel them shift and move. "Call us," I was told, "if it breaks through the skin." When I doubted that the bone would be one again, the doctor told me, "Two halves of a bone will always find each other. It doesn't matter how far away they might be."

Really? I imagined one half dropping into my left foot and a giant clavicle growing across my body like a buttress.

So I waited, and while I waited, I couldn't type or walk dogs. In other words, I couldn't do much at all. Each time I impatiently tried, I felt the bone separate again, and I reached for a bottle of wine. Brando sat in the window, waiting for anything to happen, but particularly hoping for my parents' white van to appear again, ready to take him home.

• • •

I had no interest in having a second dog until I met Zephyr, during the Time of the Broken Clavicle, and even then I had no interest. I was at a signing for my anthology *Dog Culture*, and I'd decided that it would be fun to include some foster dogs from the local Humane Society. I don't even remember the other dogs who were there, just Zephyr, a rottweiler mix who came barreling out of a station wagon and headed straight for me, dragging her foster mom along the way. "Zephyr," she yelled, trying to restrain the beast. *Who would bring an animal like that out in public?* I wondered. Minutes later the dog had climbed into my lap, where she stayed for the rest of the afternoon.

Brando had always loved rottweilers. In New York City he had a crush on a girl rottweiler named Sake who lived down the street and would growl down at us as we passed beneath the fire escape where she sat out most afternoons. On the rare occasions that Brando encountered her on the ground, he stared at her, transfixed by her beauty. Once, we found Sake waiting for her owner outside the coffee shop on 9th Street, and Brando took the opportunity to stick his tongue in her mouth. She didn't like it. Later, once we had moved to Florida, I spotted a stray rottweiler in front of the house and lured her into the yard to play with him. He chased her all around the yard, sticking his tongue in her ears, until finally she came inside and sat in front of the television to watch cartoons; she'd had enough of dogs, particularly of Brando. I discovered that her owners were the students on the fourth corner, college students who slept all day on Saturday and never knew that she had been gone so long. Her name was Brazen.

"Do you want her?" Zephyr's foster mother asked. I was teaching Zephyr "sit" and "down" as we waited for more customers at the signing.

"No," I said confidently. "But if I was going to get a second dog, I would definitely want this one."

• • •

That evening when I arrived home, Brando ran up and smelled the scent on my lap and ran to the window to see where the dog was who smelled so good. Despite my claims of disinterest, I must have been interested enough to get the number of the foster mother. I called her and we made a date.

Pam Houmere is the queen of Tallahassee dog rescuers, always with a gaggle of dogs no one else is willing to take or handle, not to mention the horses and actual geese wandering her property. She also reminded me of several people I have known in a weird dream sort of way that made her seem immediately familiar even before I could place who it was she seemed to be channeling from my past—a combination of a former babysitter from my childhood and a former student from New York, both challenging, compassionate troublemakers. Brando seemed familiar with her, too. He could be suspicious of strangers, but when Pam pulled into the drive in her red station wagon, Brando seemed to think he was meeting an old friend.

Brando and I had established a routine with visitors—we would go out to meet them in their cars first. Cars impressed him, and once he checked the tires and looked in all the windows, anyone who owned a car was okay with him. We scrambled out, and he spotted Zephyr in the back. It was more than he could take. When Pam opened the door, Brando climbed into the backseat and began licking Zephyr's face.

We coaxed them into the backyard, where Pam and I sat on the deck watching the two dogs figure out how to play. They did a couple of tentative dances across the yard together and then disappeared under the deck, where they lay together in a den Brando had dug the day before, as if he was expecting company.

"Who's that?" Pam asked. She had spotted my neighbor's dog, Katrina, who was observing the play tentatively from around the corner of a shed. Katrina spotted us watching her and promptly retreated. She was brindle, like Brando, and scrawny. Her head seemed too small and pinched; her ears stood partway up, but at a certain point gravity weighed them down. The young couple who owned her were both probably still teens. The boy bragged to me about how he had paid just $175 for Katrina, and he planned to breed her. He thought she was a pit bull, but whatever she was, she wasn't pure. He could have easily gone to a shelter and paid half the price for a better dog. The human girl half of the couple treated Katrina like a baby on the rare occasions that anyone paid attention to her. And they had just had a real baby of their own. At night I often heard them fighting over the child, but I couldn't make out the details of what they were saying all the way across our lawns.

"They leave her out there all day," I told Pam. "They barely even feed her." Katrina seemed fascinated by the fact that I spent time with my dog. She would watch us play as long as I didn't seem to know she was watching; when I did look up she would hide again. I'd fed her over the fence several times, but even when I was giving her food, she was afraid. She had obviously spent most of her life in isolation, and now she was confused about where she fit in. She seemed almost autistic: keenly aware of the world around her, but unable to interact with it.

"You could probably take her and they wouldn't even notice," Pam said, although she wasn't really suggesting it. Pam kept asking me questions about Brando, kept telling me how special Zephyr was, making it clear to me that she wasn't going to allow this dog to live with just anyone. I assumed she said this stuff to most people who were interested in taking a dog from her, to test them out and see who was willing to stick it out. She wasn't trying to sell me on Zephyr at all. In fact, she was telling me it would be a long process. She was telling me how challenging the dog might be. She didn't want to give the dog up to someone who would turn around and give up on the dog. Some rescuers will unload their animals quickly, hoping that once the dog is in a home, the relationship will stick. Others draw the process out, making sure that the dog is going to someone who isn't going to quit easily. They'll even put it in the contract: If you change your mind, if anything happens, if your situation changes and you can't keep the dog, you *will* call them.

She told me Zephyr's story, how someone had spotted her falling out of a pickup truck on the highway outside Zephyr Hills. The driver of the truck never stopped. The Samaritan picked Zephyr up from the side of the road, brought her to a vet, and then tried to drop her off at the Humane Society, where the staff were explaining that they weren't a shelter and didn't take animals from the public when Pam walked in. Perfect timing: Pam specialized in rottweilers.

The day Pam brought Zephyr for that first visit, she also had chickens in the car that were on their way to the county fair. I'd never been to a fair and neither had Brando, so the next thing I knew we were all piled in. I looked back at the dogs, huddled together on one side of the backseat. Brando wasn't letting Zephyr get too far from him. While Pam dropped off the birds, I walked the grounds with the two dogs, whom I now realized were on a date. Brando was interested in the huge steers that were lined up, getting hosed down and ready for judging later that night. He wanted to get closer to them, but was cautious—he had limited experience with any animal bigger than himself, and they were much, much bigger. Zephyr kept her eyes on the bird tent, where Pam had disappeared.

Walking two dogs is a little like flying a kite with each arm. At first it seems impossible, but eventually you learn to anticipate the wayward directions each line might take. I was still healing from the accident, though, using my one good arm and managing, almost.

We piled into the car and drove back to the house. "Let's try this again," Pam said. "And see how they do."

two or three
things about
heartworms

IN ORDER TO UNDERSTAND THE CONDITION OF MANY OF THE animals I've found, you need to understand a few things about the heartworm.

The first time I heard the word *heartworm* I thought maybe it was a heart-shaped worm, because my brain didn't want to imagine the alternative: a worm that feeds on the heart. If you grow up in the North, you don't have to know the truth, because in colder climates the chances of a heartworm infestation are small. But not impossible. In hotter climates, among strays and neglected dogs, the chances of infection are pretty good, and the cost of treating it means that many dogs are put to sleep for something that is entirely preventable.

This is how it works: Nefarious mosquitoes inject young, tiny worms into the bloodstream of the dog. The worms cling to the heart and lungs, where they grow to be up to a foot long each, and they begin to reproduce, so that more mosquitoes can transport their offspring to a new host: your dog. Once the worms have begun to tangle around the heart and respiratory system, the dog may begin to show signs of there being something wrong—coughing, breathlessness. The worms are slowly suffocating him.

It's easy to blame mosquitoes. After all, what good do they do? Without them the heartworm would be nothing—it apparently can't be transferred without spending time in a mosquito body before being passed into a dog, or cat, or horse body. They are also passed into humans, but for the most part they would rather die off than live inside our inferior bodies.

If you catch the problem early enough, there are things that can be done: Using long needles, the vet can inject the dog with an arsenic-based compound—a poison—to kill the adult worms. But there's a chance that these large dead worms will dislodge from their original location and become clogged somewhere else. Because of this, the dog undergoing heartworm treatment must be kept still for up to a month after each injection. If the dog gets too excited or sustains an elevated pulse, the force of the blood current could knock the dead worms loose into the circulatory system. Throughout the treatment, chest X-rays and stethoscopes monitor the progress of the poison and the worms. Once the first round of worms' corpses have been successfully broken down into the dog's system, more injections are performed, until no trace of the worms is found.

But it's still not over. Now attention turns to getting rid of the tiny worm ancestors that remain in the bloodstream. A year after his treatment—if he survives—the dog can be tested for the antibodies again. If he tests negative, the celebration begins.

Of course, all of this is preventable. The monthly oral treatments available don't keep the mosquitoes from injecting the worms, but they do keep the worms from growing to adulthood.

Of course, there are people who claim to care for their pets who can't be bothered with the expense of giving the monthly treatment.

Of course, these same people are likely to scoff at treating the dog if they were to get a diagnosis.

It's just worms, after all. How bad could it be?

In New York City, in winter, we didn't even bother with it ourselves. I hadn't yet moved south, where mosquitoes swarmed year-round. I hadn't ever waited through the long painful treatment with a dog, but soon I would.

endings and
beginnings

ONE OF MY FAVORITE *NEW YORKER* CARTOONS FEATURES TWO dogs sitting in front of a computer screen. The caption: "On the Internet no one can tell you're a dog." The amount of hilarity this provides me is embarrassing, but the line is endlessly clever. Is it making fun of the Net, or our fear of being judged physically? Or is it just acknowledging the willful cleverness of dogs, who would, without a doubt, love to play their practical jokes on us via the Web, if only the keyboard wasn't so difficult to negotiate with a paw?

Of course, if dogs used the Net, they would discover immediately its drawbacks: no cuddling and no treats. This would render the technology worthless. It is possible, I think, that the value of a dog's companionship has increased in the age of the Internet. Dogs continue to bring us into a real space, even as our other connections fade into the world of forwarded messages masquerading as communication.

Meanwhile, in Florida, I typed away one-handed on e-mails to my friends while Brando raced in and out of the house, occasionally bringing me his blue ball—the one that had disappeared into the river and mysteriously appeared again in the pet shop in the East Village. And Katrina watched us with suspicious curiosity, trying to figure out how this worked. Finally one day she approached the fence and bowed down at Brando. He bowed back. They bowed back and forth and raced up and down the length of the fence between them. I watched from the deck for a while and then went over to cheer her on, but she shied away from me again, and the game stopped.

Now it was my turn to hide, peeking through the door of the house while Brando continued to pursue another game with her. I e-mailed Pam to let her know the good news, and she replied, "Well, I guess if Brando has a neighbor dog to play with you don't need to take Zephyr."

I was beginning to feel that Pam didn't think we were good enough for Zephyr, or that she was testing us, to see how badly we really wanted not just a second dog, but Zephyr specifically. I kept asking for another visit with her, but our schedules didn't match. Meanwhile, the situation next door was getting worse. Fighting, yelling, one or the other of the couple storming off. One day I watched as they fought in the front seat of their car, screaming and slapping as the blond wife drove back and forth in the entry to their driveway, until finally she knocked over the mailbox and walked away with their infant son. They would disappear for days at a time, leaving Katrina behind on her own, peering around the corner from the back of the house or sometimes sitting on the porch, waiting for them to come home.

Their landlady showed up at my door one day near Thanksgiving.

"Tell them I took their dog in last night. She was shivering for an hour after I got her, she was so cold. They shouldn't have a dog; they can't even take care of that baby."

Later, I discovered that this woman wasn't just the landlady, she was also the husband's mother, but that didn't stop her from talking trash.

"If they need someone to take the dog, I could take her and find her a home," I said.

She looked at me suspiciously.

"I don't want her," I said. "But she'd be a lot happier somewhere else, and I know people who could find her a good home." Of course, I didn't really know what I was talking about. I was making the enormous assumption that I could find someone else to take care of the problem, and it all came back to me later that night, when sometime after dark there was a knock on my door and the neighbor's wife appeared with a police escort and the dog.

"I'm leaving," she said, as if we had talked this all through. The police were there to make sure nothing happened when she gathered her things. "I'm taking my baby and getting out of here. I've got a restraining order against him. I heard you offered to take the dog. I should be able to get her back after about a month. It's my son's dog, and he's not going to take her away from my son. I got that dog for my son." Her son was a couple of months old.

She disappeared and brought me a bag of crappy dog food—made with corn and "animal digest," code for any ground-up animal the manufacturer can find—and I accepted it, knowing that I'd throw it away as soon as she was gone. Then she asked if I'd look after one more thing: her hope chest, which she didn't have room for in the car. (Later, I cracked it open to see what was inside. Its totally ordinary contents depressed me. Maybe it had been a hope chest at one point, full of things that held promise and meaning; now it was just a storage container for stray appliances, a blanket, some videotapes.)

Brando thought this was an excellent plan. Katrina wasn't so sure. Playing with the safety of a fence between them was one thing; moving in together was more than she could understand. Brando pranced around doing the play-bow toward her, running up to her face, then lowering his chest to the ground in submission while keeping his back legs erect, poised for action. He was trying his best to initiate a dog game. Katrina eyed the exits and plotted her next move. Once the girl had gone, Katrina ran out the back door and began digging frantically to get under the fence. I tried coaxing her in with food. She didn't care. I tried grabbing her by the collar (she didn't have a leash—on the rare occasions they walked her, they used an old belt), and she bit me. It wasn't a real bite—she didn't break the skin—but she wanted me to know who was in charge. I was terrified that she would run away only an hour into her term of protected custody.

"I don't care if you bite me, you're coming in," I said and grabbed her again. This was a moment of complete idiocy. But it worked.

• • •

Over the next few weeks Brando was happier and calmer than I'd ever imagined he could be. Before Katrina, I would hear Brando crying when I left each morning to teach at the university. Now, with the two of them crated side by side, there were no problems at all. My clavicle was still healing, and I discovered that having a second dog took a lot of the pressure off me as well. Brando's every waking moment was directed toward her.

Sleeping arrangements were quite different. Brando established very quickly that there would be only one dog allowed in my bedroom. On one of Katrina's first days with us, I walked back to the bedroom and stepped in a cool puddle of pee just outside the door. At first I thought it was something Katrina had done as she got used to the idea of living indoors. Later I realized that it was Brando's line, the only one Katrina could not cross. When I'd picked Brando up from his shelter, I had made one rule I promised myself I would not break: There would be no dog in the bed. Within minutes of our arrival in my apartment, the two of us were curled up together, napping. I tried to keep him crated at the foot of the bed, but he would cry hysterically until the door was opened and he would leap up to the foot of the bed, curling himself into a ball as small and quiet as he could. As the months passed and he grew larger, Brando tried out a number of elaborate sleeping positions designed to create the largest common surface area between our two sleeping bodies. Eventually he had me trained: I couldn't sleep without him pressing gently along the length of my right leg. He might be willing to share the bed with other humans, but not with another dog. That was our time, and he wasn't going to give it up, not even for Katrina.

In the morning Brando would race down the hall to find her and proceed to lick her entire head, concentrating on the ears, which he'd thoroughly clean, inside and out.

I began to notice a look of extreme displeasure on her face as he did this. Katrina's eyes scrunched up and she appeared to be holding her breath, counting the seconds until the torture might be over. In the yard Brando would bring toys to her in an effort to get her to chase him. She collected the toys one by one and put them beneath a tree that she had claimed as her own. Soon he didn't even want to play fetch with the blue ball anymore, for fear, I think, that she would take it.

Katrina had no trouble with me. Anytime she could get my affection, she took it, but always on her own terms. If I was watching TV, she sat next to me. Even then, though, she would close her eyes, as if feigning unconsciousness made it possible to be close to me without fear of having to return my affection. I still didn't want to keep her, even if Brando did. I was beginning to realize that if I was looking for another dog, it wasn't just for Brando, it was also for me. A spare dog, so that if anything happened to Brando, I wouldn't be dogless, because dogless, my entire life would fall apart.

One day Brando ran up to her with a stick in his mouth. It is a classic game that seems to be programmed into dogs at birth: One dog has a stick, the others don't. The dog with the stick shows it off, and when another dog tries to take it, the stick holder pulls it just out of reach of the interloper's mouth. It is the best game ever. So Katrina went for it, Brando pulled away, and Katrina dove on top of him, grabbing his neck in her mouth and shaking.

I went bananas. I screamed for her to stop. Brando tried to pull away, but she wouldn't let go. Finally I ran over and dragged her off him, and she bit me five times up and down my arm. Then Brando grabbed her by the neck and started shaking her much smaller body in the air. "*No,*" I screamed, and he dropped her. By now blood was running down my arm, and both dogs were sitting in front of me unsure of what had just happened. I took Katrina inside and crated her. Brando came in and kissed her through the bars.

Neither dog had a mark—dogfights often sound and look worse than they actually are—but as I cleaned my wounds I realized that during the insane seconds of the fight I had only one concern: to protect my dog. My dog was Brando. I didn't regard Katrina as my own at all.

• • •

It was nearly Christmas, and I still had Katrina. After the fight, I contacted her owner, and after a promise that she would get the dog the next day, I never heard from her again. This crushed me. I was certain that I should not have Katrina in the house, but now that she had nowhere to go, I was torn.

Dogs bite. Dogs, for the most part, are farsighted. They can't see what's at the end of their nose, which is why they like to sniff around when they get close to things. They can decipher an amazing amount of information through their nose. Beyond that, they use their mouth—putting things in it, seeing what happens when they bite down. It isn't unusual, if you spend a lot of time with dogs—particularly dogs who are strangers to you—that you will one day be bitten. But dogs that are properly socialized as puppies learn bite inhibition—so even if they are mouthy, they understand how to avoid biting hard enough to draw blood. They will retreat. They might even hide under the bed, like Brando did once when, as a puppy, he bit me. But Katrina hadn't stopped, and Brando had launched into her to protect me. Again, I had done completely the wrong thing inserting myself into their fight. I might have easily been mauled. (The best way to separate two dogs in the midst of fighting is to grab them by the hips or back legs and pull them away from each other; this requires one person per dog. Pulling just one dog is likely to escalate the situation.)

Katrina's main problem was that she had never had to interact with another dog before—nor, really, with any other humans. If she had, she might have been fine. As it was, I couldn't keep her with Brando in my home. It was one thing to put myself at risk, but what would I do when I needed to leave the dogs under the care of a dogsitter? I called a trainer who had worked with Brando when we first arrived in town. "You need to put Katrina down," she said, without ever meeting her.

I talked to Pam, who also thought it sounded like a plan. Pam understood rottweilers, but she didn't understand the wiring of a pit bull, she said.

In New York I had known dozens of dogs with bigger problems than Katrina's, dogs who managed to find loving homes with people who understood their limitations. But in New York there are no yards for dogs to be left in all day—they live their lives under constant supervision and human companionship, they walk on a leash, and spend most of their day inside their own home. In other words, a city dog in many ways has an ideal life.

Meanwhile, Brando and Katrina were playing as before, but I made a point of watching every step they took along the way. No sticks, no balls, no bones. Chasing was fine, but as soon as they started lingering over a single spot, I stopped the play before any trouble began. I couldn't help feeling that I was stuck with Katrina, even though she wasn't the dog Brando and I deserved.

One night at my computer I opened a *Publishers Weekly* e-mail newsletter, expecting industry gossip about who had a new book deal and which publishing executives had been asked to clean out their desks and go home. Instead there was a brief item announcing that Lucy Grealy, a friend of mine, had taken her own life. It was the kind of news that was too personal to receive in such an impersonal manner. I had seen Lucy at a party back in New York, and she had told me that she needed to talk; there was some trouble she wanted to share. Somehow we never got together. There had been e-mails, but when it came to actually meeting in person, Lucy kept finding excuses.

I kept reading and rereading the e-mail, I kept searching for confirmation online, and at some point, without realizing it, my mind connected Lucy and Katrina in a way that made it impossible for me to consider putting her to sleep, because if Katrina was gone, that would mean Lucy was really gone, too.

Pam called with news about a rescue group in Tampa that might take Katrina. RUFF Rescue specializes in pit bulls, and Pam and the Humane Society had found someone who was willing to send Katrina with a five-hundred-dollar contribution to support her care. Katrina had a mysterious benefactor, but first she would need to be spayed.

"I don't know," I said. "I don't know what to do." I told her about Lucy.

"You can't handle this right now," Pam said. And then she made a deal: "What if I traded you Katrina for Zephyr?"

Even that didn't feel right, because I didn't trust that Katrina would exist out of my sight, either. I made an appointment to have her spayed, dropped her off, and when I called to see if she was ready to come home I discovered that Pam had already picked her up without me. She knew it was the only way she would ever get the dog out of my home, and she knew that the dog—for its own sake, as well as Brando's and my own—needed to live elsewhere. And Katrina did. She was shuffled from one foster owner to another for weeks, each time with the warning that she needed to be kept separate from the other dogs. And each time, after a period of good behavior, she would be given the freedom to roam, then something would happen and she'd move to another home.

On the day Katrina went to the vet and never came home, Brando sprawled out in the bay window of our living room and didn't get up. Hours passed. He didn't eat. He didn't play or go outside to the bathroom. The next morning he was coughing up blood. I called Pam again, and since I didn't have a car, and the streets were flooding with a December downpour of rain, Pam came to rescue us again.

Brando had been with me when I dropped Katrina at the vet, and so when I brought him in to be checked his spirits rose as we walked through the door. He looked back and forth, hoping, I think, that Katrina would still be there, waiting.

I understood the feeling. I'd been doing it for days too, Googling Lucy's name, seeing what came up, rereading the same AP obit every time it appeared. Trying to make it real. At some point that Friday before her service, her Web site disappeared, replaced by an error message: "The site you are trying to find may have moved or no longer exists. If you were brought here by a link, the link may be broken." Then that Sunday, while everyone else was gathered in New York, her site returned as if nothing had changed. She was still there in the photos. And there she was talking again about endings, in an interview with Fran Gordon, from *Poets & Writers* magazine. "I was really interested in the ways that songs ended," Lucy said. "Whether they just simply stopped or whether they tried to sum things up, whether they faded out in the middle of a line. You know, what they defined as a conclusion. Whether it was a conclusion like, 'This form has come to its natural end,' or 'We're going to just stop it right here,' and/or [whether] just stopping it at a random moment was the natural conclusion to the form."

We talked a lot about endings, Lucy and I. The trouble was always figuring out where they belonged and how to wrap things up when in life everything seemed to fade out open-ended, the way Brando and I were both waiting now, thinking that Lucy and Katrina would still somehow come back to us, when the truth was they were both gone.

Brando was a wreck—I could tell that about him easier than I could know it about myself. Nothing interested him, not food, not playing games. Even when he climbed onto my lap on the couch, the feel of my breath in his face sent him reeling. He was frantic, and I couldn't bear watching it.

On the phone with Nancy, another of Lucy's friends, I talked about how worried I was about Brando, about all of us. "Have you told him?" Nancy asked. She had been working with a pet psychic lately and believed in these things. "You need to tell him."

I don't believe that animals understand things the way we do, or that Brando understood, literally, what I was about to say. But dogs are observant, they want to make connections between the things they sense around them, and they are more closely attuned to our moods than we realize. More likely, I was the one who needed to hear it, and if Brando relaxed later, it was because I had relaxed now having finally admitted it to myself.

"She's not coming back," I told him, "but she's not really gone. She's just going to live somewhere else from now on."

Brando was quiet and still as I spoke, and when I was done, he still didn't want to look at me.

the folk art of lost
pet flyers

THEY CAN BE FOUND EVERYWHERE—NOT JUST ON THE signposts and bulletin boards of our own town, but in any city we may be visiting or passing through. The allure is always the same: someone's loss posted for the world to see.

Even when I am in a foreign city, I can't help reading them, even when I know I'll be leaving in a few hours and there's no hope for me to help locate the missing pooch. There is something mesmerizing about them, about their ubiquity, about the ways in which people make their plea. Do they list the dog's sentimental qualities, or do they list his worst traits, as if advertising the dog's faults will discourage anyone from keeping him? Do they adopt the dog's own voice, asking, "Please help me find my home"?

At least one book has been devoted to these works of art: Ian Phillips's *Lost*, which includes this bizarre classic:

LOST BLACK LAB
No collar, No legs,
NEEDS Medicine!!!
Ask for Unca Tom Jennings

"This one is a little strange," Phillips agrees. "I have a large number of pet posters which are obvious fakes which I decided not to run in the book—but this one I can't be sure about it. It could just be bad grammar—the dog may be missing one leg . . . but the 'Unca Tom' part sounds a little suspicious, too. Who knows?"

You have to hope they aren't memorials: the plea for the return of a lost "best friend." Some have photographs, others have drawings. Some include medical information, a sense of crisis that the owner hopes will speed the dog's return. Under the surface of these flyers there is always a story, something to interpret between the lines. Some share an elaborate narrative of how the dog disappeared; others are disturbingly vague, without any detail, without a photo, and you begin to think it's no wonder the dog decided he was better off on his own.

wonder when
you'll
miss me

PAM HAD TAKEN KATRINA, BUT SHE HADN'T MADE GOOD ON her promise to trade. After the vet visit, Brando and Pam had waited in the car while I picked up his medications at the pharmacy. When I returned to the car they were sitting together in the front seat. "Brando and I have come to an understanding," she said.

"Maybe Zephyr could just come visit," I suggested, once he was well. "Brando needs to play."

"Let's see how it goes," Pam said.

She and Zephyr would pull up in the station wagon, and Brando would drag me by the leash to the car, climb into the backseat with Zephyr, and begin smooching. Even Zephyr was a little overwhelmed. In the yard Brando leapt on top of her, never giving her a chance to respond on her own. It was as if he knew his time was limited, so he was throwing every move he knew at her, one after the other: pretending to pull a leg out from under her, bowing submissively and then flipping around to knock her in the face with his ass. It was like watching really bad professional wrestling.

Pam sat on the deck, observing, urging Zephyr to give Brando a hard time. "I don't know why she's acting like this," she said. Then she gasped, "It's because she likes him!" It was becoming clear that Pam was more attached to Zephyr than she had let on. Suddenly she was telling me things to discourage me. "She still hasn't learned to go to the bathroom outside," she said at one point, and I knew she was bluffing. If I was going to gain custody of her, I might have to pry the dog from Pam's cold, dead hands. "Let's make another playdate," she said again. "And see how it goes."

I was planning to go away during spring break in March, and it was already the beginning of February; I decided that if Zephyr didn't move in by mid-February, it wasn't going to happen. I didn't want a new dog having to bond with a dogsitter while I was on vacation. Looking at the calendar, I told Pam, "If she doesn't move in by February 14, I don't think it's going to happen."

As it turned out, Pam was going out of town that weekend, so she agreed to an overnight trip for Zephyr. If it didn't work out, Zephyr would go home at the end of the weekend, and none of us needed to feel bad about it. On Valentine's Day, a Friday, Zephyr got dropped off around four in the afternoon. She and Brando chased each other in and out of the house until midnight, then they headed to my room together and curled up on the bed. Brando didn't mind sharing with her at all. On Sunday, Pam called to ask when would be a good time to pick her up.

"I don't think she's going home," I told her. "I think she's staying here."

There was a long pause on the other end of the phone. "Oh," she said. And later she admitted to me that she had cried, that she always does. When you let animals into your life, even as a foster parent, you are making a promise that you will take care of them for as long as it takes, until they find a home of their own. When they finally do leave, there's a part of them that stays with you and a part of you with them.

• • •

It had been a month since Zephyr moved in, and during that time I had steadfastly refused to bond with her. She was a terrific dog and Brando loved her, but her existence in the house was something like that of a canine concubine—she was there to play with Brando and make my life easier.

Meanwhile, Pam had offered to take a rottweiler who'd been rescued from a shelter in New Orleans. The only problem was transportation. I immediately volunteered, if only so that my vacation to New Orleans had a sense of purpose. I began exchanging e-mails with Julia Lane, the woman who had found the dog in such bad shape that the staff at the shelter hadn't been able to identify the breed; after several e-mails back and forth we realized that we had another connection—Julia had interviewed me years earlier when she worked for one of the New Orleans papers and I was in town promoting a collection of stories about people with no direction in their lives. Now we had both moved on to other, more important things.

The night before I left for New Orleans, I pulled Zephyr into my lap and suddenly felt—really felt—how much I was going to miss her. It was the first moment we had shared together, one on one, since the day she climbed into my lap at the bookstore, and suddenly I was filled with regret for leaving her. Brando, the source of all my separation anxiety issues, would be fine, but I was taken aback at the feeling I suddenly had for Zephyr as well. I hadn't known it was possible.

By the time I arrived in New Orleans, the couple who'd been fostering the dog for Julia had changed their minds—they wanted to keep her until she was stronger; they had bonded with her and wanted to see it through. The entire time I was in New Orleans, I felt naked without a dog at my heel. I had rented a car to drive there and back, and on the way back I stopped at an outlet mall in Gulfport to look for socks. I am always looking for socks. I am always finding my socks in the yard, under the couch, frequently with the heels chewed out from one half of each pair. With two dogs this problem grew worse—I would look out into the yard to see the dogs facing each other on opposite ends, a sock stretched like a rubber band between them.

As I walked from the car to the little enclave of stores, a border collie ran up and poked me in the side with his paw. He sat in front of me and smiled up, pleased with himself, and somehow, in the absence of a leash or owner, I thought he must be with someone. I knelt over him to pat his head and realized his long hair was matted and tangled. The mass of fur had fooled me—his bones were palpable through his skin.

I kept going. I walked into the Gap, headed for the sock section, and then I stopped. Did I really need socks so badly that I would leave that dog behind? I reversed direction like a shoplifter and headed back to the spot where I had met the dog. He was gone. I walked around and couldn't see him. Now I was worried.

"Have you seen a black-and-white dog?" I asked a custodian.

"Oh," he said, "he's usually outside one of the shops or another."

"Does he belong to anyone?" It was a stupid question, but I was surprised by the fact that this employee was so familiar with him.

"I think so," he said confidently.

"You do?" I was incredulous, and the man seemed startled now with my questions. "You really think that dog belongs to someone? Who?"

"Oh," he said, "one of those people on those boats."

I scanned the horizon. There wasn't a boat or body of water anywhere within sight.

I found him curled up beneath a wooden bench.

"Come on," I said, and I took him by the collar and walked him out to the car. Every car we passed he tried to get in. "Not that one," I kept telling him until we reached my rental. He hopped into the backseat and curled up until we got onto the road, and then he stood and leaned over me, resting his chin on my shoulder. It was early enough that we could make it home before the vet closed, and I would leave him there until I knew what to do. During the drive I had named him Biloxi—it sounded better than Gulfport and wasn't far from the truth.

I hadn't allowed myself to remember that the drive from New Orleans is always far longer, somehow, than the drive to it. By the time we reached Tallahassee, it was dark and the vet long closed. I called Janine, the dogsitter, and told her to make sure Brando was in his crate when I got home. I told her that I had a dog with me.

"Another one?" she said, her voice rising in disbelief. I had hired her to sit with Brando while I taught long days several times a week, and then I had betrayed her by getting Zephyr. "I don't know if I'll be able to continue," she had told me when I broke the news. "Female dogs don't like me," she'd continued. "They don't like me with their male." But Zephyr was fine with her. Zephyr was fine with everything.

When we arrived home, Biloxi wouldn't even cross the threshold. He could smell that it was another dog's turf. Zephyr was ready to play, but Brando was livid with the idea that I had spent the entire weekend on vacation with this strange dog.

I put him back in the rental, where he curled up on the backseat. I called Lisa from across the street, and we stood outside trying to decide if it made more sense to let him sleep in the car or in her large fenced yard. We decided on the yard, and I watched him from my window throughout the night, as he paced the border and stared watchfully across the distance to my house.

That morning I dropped him at the vet and called Pam.

"Maybe you should get a spare crate," Pam suggested. She was beginning to suspect that I could be lured into the dog rescue world. I wasn't buying into it just yet. I searched online for a local border collie rescue group and found one in central Florida—not local, but close enough. Meanwhile, the vet had troubling news: In addition to finding several scabby wounds beneath his matted fur, they had tested Biloxi for heartworm, and the test was positive. There would be a huge expense in treating him, and there was a chance he wouldn't survive the cure.

The rescue group wanted a picture to confirm it was a border collie I had found, so I called a friend with a digital camera, and we went to the vet to take pictures as Biloxi danced around me and struggled to make tongue contact with my mouth. When we were through there, I went back home and took pictures of Brando and Zephyr posing with political signs in my yard, mouths open in mock enthusiasm inspired by the heat. Before the rental car was gone, I took the two dogs out for a ride. Once we got out onto one of the main strips, I heard a strange, rhythmic clunking sound coming from the backseat. It was Zephyr's head against the window as she jumped for every passing truck. She hadn't fallen from her owner's truck on the highway—she had jumped.

• • •

It was Saturday, March 15, and the only interesting mail was the postcard announcing tour dates for my friend Amanda's novel, *Wonder When You'll Miss Me*. "Hey Mister!" the note on the postcard read. "x A." I had spotted a stack of her books in a French Quarter bookstore, and I decided to e-mail her the great news: her beautiful postcard, her book in stores in towns she might never see. I told her about the border collie I'd picked up along the highway in Mississippi and attached a picture of my own two dogs. The photo file was huge, so I told her, "I don't know if you'll be able to open this."

Amanda had moved from New York to California a week before I moved to Florida, and after attending her farewell party I realized it would be redundant to have one of my own. If you knew Amanda, everything in your life overlapped eventually and completely. The difference was that in Amanda's life, the same things had more spark. When we first met, I was a pizza eater and she was a waitress, identities that lasted about thirty seconds before we started talking about being writers—which neither of us was quite yet. Amanda was always a step or four ahead of me, which sometimes made me jealous, but always made it clear to me where it was I wanted to be going.

Since we had both left town, Amanda took the form of a box on the upper left of my computer screen, a box named "gin-betty." She would burst onto my screen out of nowhere, asking how Florida was, how was teaching, how was the novel coming along. We were always comparing notes, pushing each other, trying out titles on each other, taking turns not being the one holding our breath about something. These little online meetings always seemed to take place on Friday afternoon, and lately, even though she had a book coming out, her main concern was her cats. One of them was sick, and she was due to be traveling a lot promoting the book. She worried that something would happen when she was gone.

Later that weekend, I found out that Amanda was dead. She and her parents had been flying a small plane between events in North Carolina, got lost in the clouds, and crashed into a mountaintop. The tragedy of Lucy's death had been that it wasn't entirely unexpected. The tragedy of Amanda's was that it would never make any sense.

I was afraid if I didn't occupy myself with something, I would lose it completely. The fact was I *was* losing it completely. I'd even had to stop a class I was teaching when I realized that I wasn't speaking to the students, but crying in front of them instead. I rode back to New Orleans a second time with some friends who were giving a reading at Tulane and stayed behind, renting a car again to drive home alone after wandering the Riverwalk shopping center, looking again for socks. *Is this what I came here for?* I wondered. *To shop at the Gap for socks?*

I was grateful for the problem of Biloxi, yet another distraction, a crisis to which I controlled the conclusion. I couldn't save Amanda or Lucy, but I could make sure Biloxi found a home.

I bought a ticket back to New York City. I called Pam.

"You can't handle this," she said and offered to pick Biloxi up from the vet, to call the rescue group, to handle everything while I fell apart on the other end. Janine came and stayed with

Brando and Zephyr, and when I called from Manhattan to see how they were doing, she told me, "Zephyr seems upset. She goes outside, but she won't step off the deck." Later, I would discover she had a urinary tract infection, a condition that recurred a week after every trip I ever made without her. She was trying to hold everything in until I returned.

In New York I returned to the small apartment where Brando and I had once lived, and with the help of my subtenant I collected the rest of my things. It didn't seem like a place I had ever lived before. No Lucy, no Amanda, and for the time being no Brando walking with me wherever I went. On the street, people asked how I was doing, unaware that I had ever been gone.

At the memorial service, Amanda's friend Kate, who had once contacted me about the dog along the river, spoke, but I couldn't say anything to anyone that night. I sat quietly, looking around the room at people I hadn't seen since Amanda's going-away party the summer before, faces I was convinced I would never see again.

I only stayed two days, and the entire time I kept seeing ghosts, images of friends who were gone, if not literally dead. On 7th Street I ran into a dogwalker with Angus, the black Lab whose entire life Brando had once coveted. In Tompkins Square I ran into Java, a Rhodesian ridgeback, another of Brando's closest friends. He recognized me immediately, and after a couple of excited kisses he paused for a moment before rubbing his face up and down each of my pant legs, from foot to thigh, beginning on the outside, then inside, then the opposite leg again. It was a letter he was writing, a message he was trusting me to carry to Brando.

• • •

This is the true story, exactly how it happened. But my memory has invented a different version, a revision that alters the order of the events slightly, like a novelist, to get closer to the truth. In this version, I meet Biloxi later, after Amanda is already gone, in that fugue state that took me to New Orleans and back, shopping for socks along the way. It makes sense that this would be how it happened, that Biloxi would be there with me, resting his head on my shoulder, guiding me safely, all the way home.

Memory doesn't just reorder events. It can make them fade, too, improbably, so that days can pass without thinking about the loss of a friend or a dog you found along the road and sent on to an unknown end. Then time brings them both back again. A year later, as I was preparing to move again, during a final visit to the vet, he told me, "I heard from Biloxi's new family," and I had to take a moment to remember who Biloxi was. "They seemed real nice, wanted to know everything about him. I think I have their information, if you want to get in touch with them."

And at home, clearing off the cluttered desktop of my computer, I found an unmarked file and clicked on it to see its contents: a picture of Amanda and her parents, smiling in front of the plane.

pit bull
puppies

THERE'S A SOUND PUPPIES MAKE WHEN THEY ARE SEPARATED from the pack, a high-pitched yelp that travels far enough to lead their mothers back to find them. It's like a siren call that isn't sounded except in that dire circumstance. Unless you are my dog Brando, in which case you drag it out well into middle age, directing it at neighbors, a master departing for work, and peanut butter biscuits that are just out of reach. I had been back from New York for a few days when I heard Brando crying out in the yard. I half expected that he might just be sitting beneath the plum tree, waiting for summer fruit. It was just March, but Brando could be impatient.

Instead, I saw him pointing toward the fence, down toward the street that ran behind our yard. There were puppies crying somewhere; I could hear them, too.

I found them scattered among the doors along the street, two or three little pit bulls at each door along the way, and finally, halfway down the street, their mother. It was the female pit from Brazen's house, and she looked scrawny and sick. She was craning her neck, as if she wasn't sure which of her puppies to rescue first. They must have all run away, and the puppies, unable to keep up, had ended up at each of the houses, not knowing the difference. Or perhaps she had gone to each door herself and abandoned a few puppies along the way. She had never been nice to me, but I immediately began to gather up the puppies, gorgeous little puppies, each with different patches of color and a blubbery little body. The mother approached to acknowledge me, then followed me along as I filled my arms with her puppies and walked with her back to her home.

Now Brando was truly hysterical.

"They're little puppies," I yelled to him, holding them out so he could see. I carried one over to him. "Do you want one?" I asked.

It was the wrong question to ask. Of course he did. Who wouldn't want a little baby pit bull?

I knocked on the neighbor's door. No answer. I knocked again. I kept knocking until one of the students came to the door.

"I think these are yours," I said.

"My roommate's," he said. "He's not here."

"Well, these puppies are scattered down the street," I said.

"That must have been the noise I heard," he said, but without any emotion. "They were locked in the other room until my roommate got home from visiting his girlfriend."

I was beginning to realize what a mistake I had made in returning them, but now it was too late. What would I do with a litter of pit bull puppies? I wasn't even sure that any of the animal rescue groups would know what to do with them. I told the roommate that the mother looked thin.

"He doesn't take care of them," he said. "He shouldn't have dogs." We finished gathering up the pups, and I went home to try to forget about it. But I couldn't help thinking that if I had just stopped and thought for a moment I could have come up with a plan. Meanwhile, the mother dog kept breaking loose to scavenge for food, and I began to feed her, bringing out a bowl of Brando and Zephyr's expensive Wellness Super5 Chicken before sending her home. She was the same dog who'd charged at Brando and me a few times when we first moved in. Now she showed no signs of aggression to me at all, but I made a point of not being friendly beyond putting the food out and walking away as she ate it. I didn't want her taking possession of me, too.

When I saw her owner again I asked how the puppies were doing and told him about finding them scattered around the neighborhood. I asked about the mother and how thin she'd become. "She's just getting her weight back," he said, and I thought about all the mammals I'd ever known to give birth and how *gaining* their weight back was never the problem.

"I've got papers for them," he said. "I'm hoping to get at least five hundred dollars for the blue one."

Five hundred dollars. That was for the expensive one. The others were less. He might make a couple of grand if he was lucky—not bad money if you aren't investing it back into taking care of the dogs, and he definitely wasn't. I hadn't yet heard the term *backyard breeder*, but that's what he was: in it for the money, breeding dogs regardless of their health or temperament, his only interest making a quick buck now and then.

• • •

A few weeks later people started knocking at my door late at night. This isn't something Brando enjoys—he knows anyone who doesn't use the bell and is arriving past bedtime doesn't belong there at all. Brando jumped into the window and the strangers didn't flinch. It turned out they were looking for the puppies and thought Brando looked pretty impressive—maybe he was the sire. They were football players from FSU, or football player wannabes, huge, bloated, steroided up, as were their cars and trucks.

We shared the same house numbers and were at the same intersection, so the mistake was understandable. But I felt guilty again telling them where to go, that the house they wanted was just around the corner. There was no point in lying—they would find it eventually on their own. At least, from what I could tell, they didn't seem interested in dogfighting. But you never know.

the paradox
of the
no-kill
shelter

WHEN I FIRST BEGAN LOOKING FOR A DOG TO ADOPT, I ENcountered the term *no-kill* for the first time. A no-kill shelter makes a commitment to any adoptable animal in its system—he will remain there, under the shelter's care, for his entire life. As I scanned the adoptable pets on Petfinder.com and visited several shelters around the city, it was a relief to know that these dogs were not relying on me to adopt them. They were safe, and so was I—safe from making a decision to take an animal I wasn't prepared for, safe from making a decision based solely on sympathy or guilt.

The decision I did finally make was no less neurotic and illogical. I adopted Brando not because I was worried he would be put to sleep, but because after several days of visiting him I couldn't stand the idea of him living with someone other than me. Within a few visits I had developed a feverish dog-crush. I didn't even like the idea of him being walked by the volunteers at the shelter. Part of this was inspired by Brando's clever ability to play hard to get. He was hard to read, full of mixed signals, happy to see me and reluctant to do anything but sit quietly at my side. My desire to bond with him was so strong that I was willing to believe the things the staff told me: that he was almost fully grown, that he was likely a Belgian shepherd. Months later, I realized that he was a Great Dane–pit bull mix, and he ultimately grew to be ninety pounds. By then it was too late, and even if he grew larger than my studio apartment there was no way I could give him up. He was mine.

But there was another dog I had looked at and rejected, because he was too big. His name was Maury, and compared with the size that Brando eventually reached, he wasn't big at all. He was more pit in his mix, was shy at the ASPCA where I visited him. He didn't seem to know what to do with himself, and his adoption card suggested that he might have issues with trusting strangers and other dogs. I wasn't ready for that, so after one visit with him, I never returned. Instead, I kept track of him via the Web site, checking each day to see if he was still there, and for the months and months that I kept up this surveillance, he was.

This was torture, and I couldn't help wondering what the dog's life would ultimately be like if he spent the rest of it in that metal cage. How adoptable would he become while confined to that space, without ongoing human interaction, surrounded by yipping, hysterical, desperate dogs? And how many other dogs were being put down somewhere because he was taking up their space? The longer he and other dogs remained stagnant in the system, the less room there was for others to take their place, and with nowhere for those dogs to go, they might be the ones put to sleep.

If you look at the statistics for many shelters, there is an interesting trick in the rhetoric they use to report their success.

On one hand they will offer the thousands of dogs that they have "rescued," while somewhere less prominently they will feature the number of animals adopted into homes. For some poorly funded, overwhelmed shelters, the adoption rate is 10 percent or far, far less, because they simply don't have the room or resources to keep any more animals around. Ask these same organizations how many adoptable animals they have had to put down and they will answer, "None." How is it possible that 90 percent of the animals are not adoptable? In some cases it is because they have been neglected or abused beyond the point of rehabilitation, but most of the time it is simply because the criteria by which they are judged assume that certain animals are harder to place; therefore, they become "unadoptable," and unadoptable animals are put to sleep. Sometimes old dogs are in this category or large dogs or dogs with special needs. Sometimes they are put in this category simply because there isn't room at the shelter for another of that kind.

This is one of the reasons that breed-specific rescue groups have sprung up, taking in animals whom they have the experience to work with and place responsibly in good homes. Many communities have foster dog programs, where volunteers take animals in, train them, love them, and then let them move into the right home.

Of course, there's nothing wrong with shelters and other organizations setting limits on themselves. If they don't have the resources to responsibly place large-breed dogs, they shouldn't feel guilty for not taking them in. The problem is that many organizations are embarrassed to admit that they have any limitations at all. They will publicly welcome all breeds, while privately prioritizing only certain sizes, ages, and breeds. Even an organization like PETA chooses to advocate on behalf of only select animals. One of PETA's agenda items is the extinction of problem breeds like the pit bull; the claim is that making them extinct is the only way to protect the animals from abuse. Apparently the problem of abuse is not one that involves the behavior of the abusive human. Following this line of "ethical" thinking, the problem of divorce should be solved by banning marriage, and child abuse is best addressed by euthanizing children.

When I first read of PETA's hope to ban certain breeds of dogs, I contacted them, thinking that I had misread their policy. "Don't worry," they told me. "We won't take your dogs away from you." But they did confirm their firm belief that the breeds should be made extinct. This ignores the fact that making the breed illegal will simply drive up the demand for badly bred breeds, and that abusive owners will simply get another dog if their preferred breed is unavailable. But groups like PETA and others continue to spend valuable time and resources addressing the problems of the dogs, rather than the problems of the humans who choose to abuse and misbreed them.

• • •

Of course, what would I have done if on meeting Maury I had learned there was an execution date hanging over his head? Would my guilt have led me to bring him home, even though I knew he wasn't the right dog for me, and I wasn't the right person for him? Perhaps the greatest frustration with all of these theories of kill or no-kill is that no theory will stop the steady influx of unwanted animals who need to be dealt with—most coming from people who have bred their dog and don't know what to do with the offspring, or have decided that feeding and caring for an animal is more than they can manage anymore. It is a problem of human responsibility, and no amount of theories or number crunching can solve the moral disconnect that allows people to think they're above taking responsibility for the living things around them—not just their own life, not just their family, not just their friends.

valentino

A YEAR AFTER BILOXI, ON VALENTINE'S DAY, I WAS HEADED west on I-10, to New Orleans again, and feeling a little guilty, since it was Zephyr's one-year anniversary. People say that dogs have no sense of time, that they never know whether you've been gone for a few minutes or hours or days. I disagree with this idea completely—at least with my dogs, the level of enthusiasm on my return rises in proportion to the length of time I've been gone. Even with other folks' dogs, like Java in New York, there is a degree to which while they may not know how long it has been, they do know that it has been too long. Despite this, I am certain dogs do not understand the concept of anniversaries. I kept reminding myself of this as I passed the outlet where, a little less than a year before, I had found Biloxi. I had passed it many times in the year since I had found him, but I made a point not to ever stop there again.

I was meeting friends from New York in New Orleans, Ben and Sharyn, and for a while Sharyn and I had been estranged, so it was worth putting dog anniversaries on hold to meet up with them again. In a way, it had been Amanda's memorial that had made us friends again. Although we had never talked about it, or the reason for our not speaking for so long, it suddenly seemed clear, that night, that few things in life are as important as friendship. Except, maybe, dogs.

I pulled into a truck stop just past Gulfport, because I didn't want to be stuck with an empty tank as soon as I got to town. On the way back from paying, I spotted a beautiful fawn-colored eighty-five-pound pit bull sitting patiently outside the station, and I watched as he scampered after a customer. The dog walked alongside the man, sat patiently as the car door was opened, then watched as the car pulled away from him. The dog returned to sit outside the station door and followed another customer to his car. Each time I thought, *This must be the owner.* Yet, as each of them drove away, I began to suspect that the dog didn't have an owner at all. On the other hand, he was too well behaved to have been abandoned—not that people who abandon dogs need a good reason.

I continued to watch him as he followed customers back and forth from the pumps to the register. I saw him walk one man out to his truck and then accompany him as he maintained each part of the truck. "Is that your dog?" I asked. The man shook his head no. The dog went over to the weighing station and seemed to be craning his head to look into the cab of the truck there, but that driver returned and left without him, too. I headed back into the station and asked, "Does anyone belong to that dog out there?"

"Someone dropped him off this morning," the cashier said.

"So I can take him then?"

"If you want him, sure."

When I came back out, he was gone. Part of me was relieved, but another part knew that I would continue to wonder what had become of him, so I kept looking. "He went over there," someone said, pointing toward the embankment down to the highway. I looked over the guardrail, and there he was, wandering alongside the traffic exiting I-10. I climbed over the rail and down the muddy embankment after him.

This is not what you should do when you spot a dog along the road. But the closer I got to him, the more frightened I was at what might happen if I didn't get him away from the road. Fortunately, he was thirsty and drinking from a mud puddle, so I managed to catch up to him and take him by the collar.

Don't ever take a strange dog by the collar. It puts your hand and arm directly in range of his mouth. I sensed, against sense, that I had nothing to fear in this case and led him back up the hill and into my van. I can't remember why I didn't put him into the back of the van, where I actually have a dog grid set up to keep the animals in the cargo area. He settled into the passenger's seat, and I pulled onto the highway, talking to him the entire time. After a few minutes he began leaning toward me. Then he put a paw on my lap. Next he was sitting on top of me, turning to face me, and settling down with his back to the road, his face staring directly into mine.

I couldn't even see the road. "What are you doing?" I asked, nervous, a little, to find out. I didn't think he would attack me, but we were in a closed-in space, on the road—not a place to find out. Out came his tongue, and the kisses began. Now I was laughing, and still unable to see where I was going.

"You're going to have to go back to your seat," I said, not expecting him to listen. Yet he immediately went back to the passenger's side and stayed there for the rest of the drive to New Orleans. At this point I was late and was due at lunch with my friends. I called from the car to tell them the news.

"I may be a little late," I said. "There was a pit bull at the gas station . . ."

"What did you do with it?" my friends asked, probably aware of what the answer would be.

"He's here with me in the car."

"We aren't ever going to see you, are we? You're going to spend the weekend with that dog."

"I'm just running late," I said.

I tried calling other friends, who lived in New Orleans, and kept getting machines. "Hi," I said in their voice mail, "I just drove into town, and I found a terrific pit bull. I'm trying to find a place he can stay, maybe just for a few days . . ." No one picked up. No one returned the call. And really, who can blame them?

The Louisiana SPCA is open seven days a week, and it is nearly always bustling with action. The dog was excited as we drove through the city and whimpered a little at the sight of dogs being walked just outside his window. I had decided to name him Valentino, because of the holiday, and because I hoped that a pit bull with a romantic name might get better treatment in the shelter. Better, certainly, than "Stray Pit Bull." The woman at the front desk patiently answered all my questions about what would happen to him after I left and told me that he would be held in quarantine for five days before he was adoptable, that I wouldn't be able to visit him during that time, that pit bulls were hard to place, and that for a ten-dollar fee they would call and notify me if he was going to be put down. She told me all of this between answering the phone, tending to other walk-ins who were either looking for a dog or wanting to drop one off or, in one case, hoping to trade one in for a smaller model. Every time we were interrupted I tried calling people again to find him another temporary home. Meanwhile, Valentino sat patiently at my feet, watching all the action around him.

Finally I signed him over, and the woman at the desk said, "We don't do this, but if you want you can come with me and check him in." I wasn't concerned about the people or the facilities. My concern was the dog himself. I had no idea what he had experienced in his life or how he might respond to being shut into a kennel. I wanted to see for myself how he took it, so I could fight for him later, if it came to that.

At the time I had no idea why I felt so committed to him, so certain that he was worth whatever it might take to save him. The answer, of course, was Rocco.

Valentino behaved beautifully, following all of our cues down a narrow corridor, into a room where he quickly received shots and a worming treatment from a team of vet techs who clearly had the system down—who holds the dog, who gives the shots, who squirts the worming liquid in his mouth and sends him on his way. Next, we walked through the kennel, and Valentino ignored the barking dogs along the way to settle into his own little space before yelping a little as I forced myself to walk away. I told the volunteer that I was worried about the other dogs, that if they weren't friendly Valentino might respond—if they barked at him, he might bark back and then be labeled as a troubled dog. Everything I had seen from him suggested that he was no trouble at all, but that didn't mean that in a kennel environment things might not change.

From the SPCA I went straight to the Three Dog Bakery on Royal Street, to order a cake for Brando and Zephyr, a giant frosted peanut butter bone decorated with their names. We would celebrate the anniversary, I decided, as soon as I got home.

• • •

The following day was the Barkus parade, an annual dog parade through the French Quarter that raises money for local animal groups. I had been to one of the first ones, ten years earlier, with a handful of people parading their dogs through the Quarter. I wasn't prepared for how large it had grown: They now limited registration to a thousand. There are floats, canine grand marshals, lavish costumes. The theme that year was the Wild West, and the parade began with men dressed as horses pulling tiny stagecoaches driven by Chihuahuas in cowboy hats and plaid shirts. Although we hadn't made strict plans, my friends knew that if they stood in front of the Three Dog Bakery long enough they would run into me. When I picked up the dog cake Ben asked, "Do you really think the dogs will know whether or not you had their names put on it?" Sharyn was more supportive of the idea, insisting that I open the box and show the cake off for her camera while we sat in a bar ordering drinks.

After Barkus, I went back to the SPCA, where they broke the rules again and let me visit with Valentino. He seemed happy to see me and sat at attention as soon as I appeared. He had obviously been trained by someone, and yet here he was. Did his owner get tired of him? Had he done something wrong? Could someone not realize this wonderful dog was missing?

On the way back to Florida, I began to drive off at each exit in Mississippi, looking for the truck stop where I had found this little man. When I finally found it, I went in to ask if anyone had come back looking for their dog. No, they hadn't. On the way out, I looked up to get the name of the station to add to the dog's file at the SPCA.

It was at Love's Truck Stop that I met Valentino. It was like something out of a Tennessee Williams play.

• • •

I was teaching an essay course and spent a few minutes of each class session telling stories, partially to warm up the class, mostly because the students were rarely there on time and I hated repeating important information. There were a lot of dog stories told, and the students knew to at least pretend to be interested, but when I told them about Valentino, they didn't hold back their groans when I mentioned his name. I e-mailed everyone I could think of to ask for their help finding him a home. I e-mailed Julia to let her know about the dog, hoping that even though he wasn't her breed (her specialty being shepherds) she might be able to get the word out. A few days later Julia e-mailed a whole series of portraits she had taken at the shelter. She said he was doing great. Valentino looked like a king in the pictures, standing proudly, showing off his posture and physique.

Yet a few days later, eight days after I had dropped him off, I arrived home to a message from the SPCA telling me that he would be put to sleep if I didn't come get him that day. I hate to use the phrase *my heart stopped*—unless I literally mean it—but that was how I felt when I heard the words. He had only been up for adoption for two days.

I called and spoke with the same staff member who had been so helpful to me before. "I really don't know why he got tagged," she said. "There's a note on here about aggression. But I never saw anything in his behavior that would suggest he was aggressive. I can have the volunteer who made the note call you," she added. "We can hold him until the end of the week, if you are certain you will get him."

I was certain I would get him. I just didn't know how—I had to work all week, and it would be at least a twelve-hour trip to pick him up and a problem bringing him into my home. Even if they performed the procedure, Brando would likely smell Valentino as unaltered, and that would be trouble. But I could work something out, I was sure.

I called Julia to ask why she hadn't said anything about there being a problem. She said she didn't think there had been a problem. Another volunteer had brought out an unaltered bullmastiff, she said, and as they stood facing each other in an enclosed courtyard space, Valentino had growled at the dog, but she hadn't thought anything of it. It seemed to her a typical reaction for dogs who had only recently been sheltered: two males, completely unfamiliar with each other, acting defensively. "The reason I didn't tell you," she said, "was that I really didn't think it was a problem."

I could understand the SPCA's concern as well. They didn't have room for all the dogs they received, so why would they bother to work with a dog who might have issues? Nor could they be certain those potential temperament problems wouldn't manifest themselves if they adopted the animal out. Yet I had spent an afternoon with Valentino, and it was long enough to know that he deserved a home.

• • •

My students gasped when I announced the news the following day, although most of them were probably humoring me, in it just for the grade. I told them that he was being held there, and that I needed to find a way to get him before the end of the week. One girl raised her hand and said, "I'll go."

"Are you serious?"

"I've been wanting a second dog," Victoria said.

"But you haven't even met him."

"I've heard everything you've told us in class. He sounds like a good dog. I've seen his picture. He has good posture."

I was skeptical. I was sure that Valentino would make a good dog, but I wasn't sure he would make a good *second* dog. Still, I was stuck, unable to clear my schedule or get a dogsitter in time to meet the deadline. I printed out a map and signed an adoption agreement via fax. I told the SPCA that Victoria would be transporting the dog for me, but not that the dog might very well end up hers.

On the day that Victoria and her boyfriend drove to pick him up, I found myself wondering, *What have I done?* What if the dog wasn't stable? What if he had become apprehensive during his time in the shelter? Victoria and her boyfriend would be in their small car with him for six or seven hours on the return trip. She called the following afternoon. "I was worried," she said. "But everything is fine. He loves my other dog. It's like they've known each other all their lives."

● ● ●

I visited their apartment a week later, to see Valentino again and check up on all of them. I knew Victoria was like me: likely to want things to work out and to ignore the possibility that things could go wrong, the way I had been with Katrina. I also knew that as sweet as she was, Victoria's situation wasn't exactly what

I had in mind. But she had been the one who was able to retrieve him from the shelter, and if she wanted to keep him now, I wasn't sure I could find good reason to deny her claim.

The apartment was tiny, a living room and kitchenette with a bedroom off to the side. I sat on the couch, and Valentino came closer to smell my feet. He looked up into my eyes and climbed halfway into my lap before stopping himself. He leaned forward and kissed me. He danced around my feet.

"I told you," I said. "I told you I'd get you out."

Behind the bedroom door I could hear the younger dog whining.

"She's a little crazy with guests," Victoria said.

"Go ahead," I said. "Let her out." I wanted to see the dogs play together.

The girl dog—a crazy terrier mutt—raced into the room and took Valentino's place at my feet. She peed on the carpet.

"I'm so sorry," Victoria said. "She's never done that."

The dog jumped up and peed on my lap.

"Oh my," Victoria said.

"It's okay," I said. "She's just jealous." Now she had Valentino's attention. The two of them raced around the house. Valentino rolled over on his back and let the girl dog climb on top of him. Within a few minutes he was exhausted and flopped into a corner of the room where she couldn't get to him. He needed a rest.

Victoria's boyfriend came home, and Tino, as they now called him, settled at his feet. A neighbor stopped by and Tino greeted him. He respected everyone and everyone treated him with respect. I was jealous that they were going to get to spend his whole life with him, but I knew that this was best.

After a while, I decided it was time to go. As I walked down the apartment corridor, I could hear Tino whining behind their door.

I never saw him again.

how to
let go

First accept that no list will really help you.

Your job is to get the dogs ready for their real home. Focus on socializing them with the outside world rather than cuddling with them in front of a fire.

Only adopt to people you feel are right for the dog. Encourage them to keep in touch, but allow them room to have the dog on their own terms.

Keep photos. Pam told me to start an album of photos. You might not want to look back at them, but at least you know they are there. There will be times you need to remind yourself: This is why we do it.

Every dog you place opens up room for you to help more.

Remind yourself, if you have to, the dog was never really yours.

the dog who
found me

ON ST. PATRICK'S DAY MORNING, BRANDO WAS OUTSIDE IN the yard again, crying. Through the fence and the overgrown bushes outside it, I could see the shadow of a black dog scampering across the street. We had another set of new neighbors down the street, and like most of the college students in the area they let their dogs run freely. When they were gone, one of their dogs had been escaping by jumping through a broken window, and once he was free he'd sit in the empty jeep parked in their drive, or pace back and forth at the edge of the road, warning everyone to stay away. They were another example of why most college students shouldn't have dogs. They weren't bad dog owners, but their erratic schedules were putting the dogs on edge.

I threw on some clothes and went outside, where the dog was sitting on the neighbor's porch, patiently waiting. But it wasn't my neighbor's dog. It was too small, and it was a pit bull.

"Get over here!" I yelled, as if she was an old friend, and she came running. She pounced playfully in front of me, and I saw for the first time that she was in terrible shape. She was obviously still just a puppy, black with a white tuxedo chest and gloved hands, but her face was freshly wrecked. There was a straight line cracked open across the bridge of her nose, and her right eye was nearly out, the red flesh of its socket hanging out from behind the eye itself. Still, all she wanted to do was play. She had a heavy orange collar that made her look like livestock; there were no tags to let me know where she belonged. And anyway, it looked like she had been used in a fight.

I tied her to a pole under the carport, then went back into the yard where Brando was feeling left out. Zephyr, as usual, continued her hunting, unaware that she would soon lose her title as the only woman of the house. Once I had lured the dogs back inside to their crates, I took the little pit bull to the car and drove her over to the vet. The whole way there she kept trying to climb into my lap, turning to kiss me, and with each kiss she brought that horrific torn eye socket into my view, close up.

"That's okay," I told her. "We don't have to kiss." I was on my way to teach, so I dropped her off at the vet, who by now was used to my appearing with strange dogs who were only temporarily mine. My file was filled with various dummy accounts: "Stray dog," "Stray pit bull," "Stray Lab," et cetera. When I got to class, I told them the latest news. I had found a stray pit bull.

"In New Orleans," they said, bored with the story of Valentino.

"No, outside my house," I said. "This is another one."

* * *

The vet let me know three things: She was in heat, she was heartworm-positive, and she would likely need surgery on the eye. Also, she was incredibly even tempered and was probably about a year old. "She's a good dog."

I began calling around to see who would take her. I knew that if I took her up to the shelter, a pit bull with her face torn up, the chances of her lasting more than a day were pretty slim. I called the Leon County Humane Society, and the person on the phone told me that they didn't take animals from the public, which was strange since they had been happy to help when I'd found a yellow Lab a few months before. I called Pam, knowing that the last thing she wanted was another dog from me, but that she would probably still be willing to help. And I called a new group, Extended Circle Animal Haven, and told them that whatever they could do was great, but what I really needed was to find a way of paying for the treatment. Extended Circle was trying to raise money to start an animal sanctuary where strays could be housed indefinitely. The members didn't have an office yet, so like a lot of animal groups they relied on people fostering dogs in homes, and e-mail communication. It was a little difficult at first trying to track someone down.

"Can you e-mail a picture?" they said. "I think we know someone who can help."

During all this time, she still didn't have a name, and none of my previous naming tricks seemed right. Should I name her Pat for St. Patrick's Day? No. And certainly not Neighbor's Front Porch. I kept calling her "lady," which was beginning to seem rude. I tried Lucy, but that didn't seem right. Finally Sula came out of my mouth, and it stuck. I liked it: distinctly female, but strong, which is what she would need to be if she was going to get through all her treatments.

I took Sula that night to a friend's house to get some quick digital pictures done. "She can't be a pit bull," she said as Sula bombarded her with kisses. "She's too nice!"

"This is a pit bull," I said, and I meant the kisses.

• • •

I placed an ad in the local paper. "Dog Found. Black, young female." I made a point of not saying *pit bull* because if I had, all kinds of people would have come forward claiming to own her. If someone was looking for her, "black female" would be enough. There was only one response, from an older woman whose voice had the dry sound of desperation.

"I'm looking for an older male dog," she said. "I know your ad said it was a young female, but I was hoping maybe it was a mistake." She paused. "I don't know what I'm going to do if I don't find him."

"I'm sorry," I said. "Have you called the local vets? Maybe they've seen him."

Barbara Law, my contact at Extended Circle, e-mailed me back and let me know that there was a woman who would pay Sula's medical expenses on the condition that we use her vet, where an account was already set up. Of course, I had no problem with that—all I cared about was getting the dog well again and finding her a home.

At my place I was still keeping her separated from the other dogs. I didn't want them to get her excited, but more than that I didn't want them to get attached. Also, I didn't want her bleeding all over the house. I had never been near a dog in heat before, and I'd had no idea how messy it can be. Naturally, Brando was fascinated and wanted to lie as close to Sula's crate as possible, deliriously staring at her until Zephyr came over and sat on him. *Remember me?* Zephyr seemed to be saying.

Sula was very pleased with herself. Even with all her health problems, even confined to a tiny cage borrowed from another set of neighbors down the street, she lay back completely relaxed, as if she had known this was where she would end up. Or perhaps she was exhausted from her long journey.

I was determined to keep the dogs apart, even if she was going to stay during the treatment. While the other dogs were in the backyard, I would take Sula into the front, where she would do her business and then gently stand on her hind legs and hug me, pressing her head to my stomach. Then I would lift her into my arms and she would wrap her front legs around my neck and stay there, her back legs dangling at my waist. I held her like that, standing at the edge of our drive, and then I reminded myself that she wasn't mine and she wasn't staying.

• • •

All my own animals had come to me with names, already neutered, healthy. Now, with a dog I had no intention of keeping, I was waiting for the vet to call, to let me know the surgery went well. They had to decide which procedures to do first: recutting the torn inner lid of her eye, spaying her, or treating the heartworms. They settled on doing the surgical procedures first, then moving on to the more complicated treatment for heartworms. By now I had read about the treatments, and I had known dogs, like Biloxi, who had come through the treatments without complication, but I hadn't ever gone through it myself—dropping the dog off, waiting for the call to pick her up, and waiting for the poison to do its work, all the while hoping that nothing went wrong, that the giant worms were killed and would deteriorate slowly, without stopping her heart.

The key, as I've mentioned, is to keep the dog from moving, so there is no danger of accelerating the pumping of her heart. Sula stayed in a crate the whole time, waiting three weeks before going in for a second treatment and then staying in the crate another three weeks again. We went outside to go to the bathroom and then turned around and went back to the crate. She never complained, she never resisted. Meanwhile, I had to keep myself from gasping melodramatically each time the vet told me that it looked good, that she probably would make it through okay. *Probably?* I thought she was already through the hard part.

In addition to the surgical procedures, there were pain pills and courses of antibiotics that followed each procedure, as well as worming her several times when I found evidence of different parasites in succession: tapeworms, roundworms, and so on. All of this was costing in the thousands of dollars at this point, and because I didn't know who was paying for it, I felt hesitant each time I needed something for her. First I would e-mail Barb Law at Extended Circle, then she would forward my request to the sponsor, then the sponsor would tell her what to tell me about getting whatever it was I needed. At one point I ran out of food for all of the dogs and was between paychecks with an empty checking account. Barb arranged a food drop-off to tide us over until my paycheck arrived.

Each time I asked for help, I cringed with the anticipation that I was asking for too much, that my someone would tell me I was being irresponsible, that I shouldn't extend myself beyond my means, that I needed to be more reasonable, less needy. This never happened.

To keep Sula occupied during her recovery, I began to teach her basic commands. To sit for a treat. To lie down. This she loved, and sometimes her enthusiasm led to her repeating the sequence on her own, without the commands, just to get my attention. Up, sit, down. Everything between us became a ritual. Pills, the quick trips to the front yard, the drive to the vet with her settled into my lap, then more pills. There was an intimacy between us that the other dogs didn't share.

Sula had fears. One day I picked up a small stick while we were playing, and she immediately dropped to the ground. Thunder terrified her: If it was cloudy or damp she wouldn't set a single paw outside the door. She was easier around women than men, whom she approached quickly, running back and forth between me and them until she was sure they wouldn't hurt her.

She loved the vet. Every time we visited, she would go to the bathroom outside, then run in and wait for her greeting. "Sula is here!" someone would shout, and then each of the staff would say hello as Sula ran back and forth, standing and resting her head every couple of feet along the reception desk. One morning as I was dropping her off, they told me: "Her sponsor was wondering if you want to keep her. She told us to tell you that if it's a financial question, she'll be happy to keep paying her expenses. For the rest of her life."

"Who is this sponsor?" I asked.

"Her name is Debbie Geiger."

"I'd like to talk to her," I said. And then I went home to Google her. I found an e-mail address for her and sent along a message introducing myself and thanking her for everything she had done for Sula. She called me from some remote location, where she was leading a group of travel writers on a junket. "I'm calling from a phone booth, because there is no cell reception here," she explained.

She reiterated the offer. She would pay for everything: food, vets, boarding when needed. I felt a wave of guilt and depression, because it wasn't just financial. I really didn't want a third dog. Two was perfect. Two left room for temporary dog visitors. Three made it impossible for me. ("Everyone has their limit," Barbara Law told me, adding, "Mine is thirteen.")

"I have a bunch at home already," Debbie explained. "If I could take more in, I would. But I'm never home, so this is what I do. There are about twenty dogs I take care of this way." Pit bulls.

I asked why she did it. Why pit bulls?

"I woke up one night and knew this was something I needed to do."

I told her I didn't think that I was the right situation for Sula, but that I would hold on to her until something better came along.

"You know . . . I've met her," she said. "I was at the vet one day when she was there, and they invited me back to see her. That's why I want you to keep her. They told me she seems to have a bond with you, and when I met her, well, she seems special."

"How?" I asked. I wanted her to articulate what I could not.

"We could send her to a rescue group and she would be fine, but I would feel strange not knowing where she was or who she was with."

"Me, too," I confessed.

I did research online to see if I could find a rescue group that would take her, and instead I found Pit Bull Rescue Central (www.pbrc.net), a clearinghouse of listings for pit bulls all across the country, all in need of homes, most with horrific histories of abuse. The Web site, completely volunteer-run, offers information on the breed, on what to do if you have found a pit bull, and on how to test a dog's temperament; it also stringently screens applicants trying to adopt one of the listed dogs. To list a dog, you have to fax the vet records, including proof that the animal has been spayed or neutered. I have never seen so thorough a site—and all of the "staff" got involved with the breed the same way I did: by finding a stray pit bull whom no one else would help with or take off their hands.

• • •

Once she was better, I began taking Sula for short walks, but never too far. Just as I didn't want my dogs to bond with her, I didn't want her to bond with me. Of course, this was silly considering all the time we had spent going to the vet together and all the care I had taken, feeding her, giving her the pills. I began to wonder if it might be better to let her and the dogs play together. The segregation wasn't teaching her anything, and my job was to prepare her for life on the outside. So I began to let her out, on a leash, in the yard with the others. She headed straight for Brando every time, and he couldn't have been happier. He toppled over in front of her, and Sula leapt from one side of him to the other, and Zephyr ran over from whatever she was doing to take the leash in her mouth and lure Sula away.

When you get a second dog, a certain amount of the workload is taken from you. They entertain each other. They chase each other instead of you taking them out for a walk. With three, there is a constant jostling for order among the pack. Brando was the pack leader as far as I was concerned, but the girls didn't agree with this theory. They ate his food, and he let them. They got fat, and he let them. They wrestled him for attention, and he loved it. It was total chaos, but it was fine as long as I was able to mediate among them.

When I needed to go out of town, Sula would go to stay at the vet, while Brando and Zephyr stayed at home with the dogsitter. It was one thing for me to deal with it; I didn't want to expect anyone else to juggle three dogs. Certainly not these three. When I returned from a trip, I would go first to the house and spend a few hours just with my own dogs, then back to the vet to pick up Sula. When the two of us walked through the door together, Brando would collapse onto the floor of his crate, as if I was offering the world's best treat.

After the morning wrestling matches, Sula and I would sneak away for our walk.

"Are you keeping her?" my neighbors asked one morning as we walked past their house.

"No," I said. "Just until she gets better."

"Isn't she better now?" they asked.

"Well," I said. "Yes, but . . ."

"You're keeping her," they told me. "We tried to feed her," they said, referring back to when I had found her sitting on their porch on St. Patrick's Day. "She wouldn't come near us."

"Really?" I said. "How long was she hanging around here?"

"A couple of days," they said. I wondered why she would wait so long, if she didn't belong to anyone in the area, and if she wasn't interested in taking anyone's food.

Cars slowed down whenever we were out walking. Windows rolled open. Drivers would ask, "What bloodline?" I'd tell them I didn't know. "You want to breed her?" No, I would say, she's just going to be a pet. "What a waste." Then they would roll up their windows and drive away. Apparently the only value of a female pit bull is her breeding and her ability to make puppies to sell. I wondered if these people valued women in a similar way.

I had already started trying to find her a home. I had planned to list her with Extended Circle, since they had managed to find her sponsor and get her well. None of their adoption days fit into my schedule, so I took her for a trial run at PETsMART, with the Humane Society and Pam. Sula ran and jumped and nuzzled and bowed—all like a maniac let loose after a long period in isolation. She wouldn't sit still. I walked her around the store. We looked at dog food. She checked other customers' carts to see what they were getting. Occasionally we would go back to the adoption table and sit down, but then she wanted to play with the other dogs, and I still wasn't sure what she knew about playing.

Pam was there with a dog named Toby who was the spitting image of a young, blond Brando. "Will he get bigger?" someone asked. "I'm not sure," Pam said.

"He will," I answered.

A little girl came over to Sula and said hello. Sula stood and placed her paws on the girl's shoulders, preparing to move in for a smooch. "You need to sit down," the little girl said. Sula sat immediately and waited for her next instruction.

Someone else asked, "Is this dog up for adoption?" and without thinking I said, "I don't know."

I don't know? What I meant was, I didn't know if she was ready to go anywhere that day. Or maybe what I meant was that I wasn't sure I was ready to let her go. I tried to take a break and get lunch while someone else held her, but I could hear her crying from the other side of the store. I walked back and Sula leapt into my arms. "I think she and I can go eat lunch together outside."

Later in the day Sula kept making me take her through the aisles of the store, then back to the booth, then outside, then back through the store. Each time I thought she needed something. Maybe she needed to go to the bathroom. After about the fifth trip outside I realized what she wanted. She was looking for Toby and Pam, who had already gone.

• • •

I began to notice that whenever I took Sula into the front yard, she kept a close eye on that corner house, the one with the same street number as ours, the one where Brazen had lived and the pit bull puppies had been for sale. One day some of the new tenants came out and were talking among themselves in their driveway, next to their cars. Sula crouched as flat to the ground as she could, hoping they wouldn't see her. It was then that I realized where she had come from. I walked with her across the street to the guys; she sniffed cautiously at their feet, then, not smelling what she expected, she rose to greet them.

"Nice dog," one of them said.

"I found her," I said. "I think she might have come from your house. From that litter of puppies last year."

"That guy doesn't live here anymore," they said.

"Oh," I said. "But she's the right age, isn't she? Your neighbors told me that she'd been hanging out for a few days before I took her in."

"I don't know what that guy did," one of the guys said. "But I guess there was something wrong with those puppies. People kept coming back looking for him."

I wondered if they all had heartworms or if it was something worse. I was certain now that whatever had happened to her, Sula had come back looking for her mother, but instead found me.

what Zephyr
dogs do when
they need
some attention

_____

1. Make snow angels in the mud.

2. Once muddy, roll around on the couch.

3. Offer to lick people dry when they get out of the shower.

4. Tilt head and stare until the message is conveyed: *This is serious!*

5. Tilt head again in the opposite direction.

6. When asked to drop it, swallow a live rat whole.

7. Place nose on edge of bed and wait for invitation.

8. Once invited into bed, tilt head and stare.

9. See number 7.

10. Once in bed, try each corner to see which is best.

11. If no one is watching, bring the biggest tree branch available into the house.

12. Dance!

the problem
with
my heart

By July we were moving again, this time to Mississippi, to go back to school again, this time for a PhD, and it was clear that, like it or not, Sula was coming with us. She had survived her eye surgeries and her heartworm treatment and then consistently required medical treatment for an assortment of other ailments, most of which she had probably been carrying when she found us: pinworms, hookworms, tapeworms . . . these would show up, one after the other, as if having eliminated one parasite gave the next one room to take hold. She also developed a rash all over her white chest, like acne visible from under her fine, thin coat of hair.

I almost got rid of her.

For ten days in July, Sula lived with a student named Jeremiah, who for some reason volunteered to take care of her while I was out of town. Brando and Zephyr would get to play with their own dogsitter during that time, and what I was hoping for was that Jeremiah would fall in love. Sula required a lot of supervision and college students are notoriously irresponsible (animal shelters are filled every spring with the pets students get rid of in time for summer vacation), but Jeremiah was a serious guy. If he wanted to take Sula, I would trust him.

A few days into my trip I got the call:

"When are you getting back?" Jeremiah asked, even though he already knew.

"What do you mean?"

"She's really high-maintenance," he said. When I returned at the end of the week, he offered more details: She didn't like being left alone; she was awful on a leash.

"Well, she's only recently been allowed to go for walks at all," I said, defending her enthusiasm.

"She's a good dog," Jeremiah conceded. "I mean, she's good to sleep with once she finds a spot."

"You let her sleep with you?" I asked, my voice rising in disbelief.

"Well, yeah."

"What else did you do?"

"I brought her some prime rib from the restaurant," he said. "She really enjoyed that."

"So you fed her prime rib and slept with her, but now you're complaining that she's too high-maintenance and expects too much?"

"Well, yeah," Jeremiah said. I wondered if it was a pattern with Jeremiah, but mostly I was worried that I was getting a spoiled dog back.

We had also visited with Extended Circle at one of their adoption days, but Sula found the setup unacceptable. While the Humane Society was able to keep dogs on leashes, Extended Circle was at a venue that required that all the dogs be caged. In order to show as many dogs as possible, the cages were stacked on top of one another, and Sula was placed in one at the bottom of the heap. She was crying, barking, hysterical. She wasn't going to make anyone's choice under these conditions, so I bought her a new collar and we left. We made one more attempt with the Humane Society, at a Bastille Day celebration at a fancy restaurant called Chez Pierre.

Sula was a hit with the children. With kids around, her whole demeanor slowed. They fascinated her; she was watchful, as if she understood exactly how deserving they were of her awe. Then the parents would arrive. Watching their children pet her, they'd ask, "What kind of dog is she?"

"She's a pit bull," I told them, making sure to say it as matter-of-factly as I could. But no matter how I said the words, the parents always took the children by the hand and led them away. People hear about pit bulls, but often they have no idea what they really are—that they used to be considered nanny dogs, trusted members of the family. Or that even when they do have issues, it's not with people but with other dogs. The breed may attract a higher number of dubious owners, but the breed itself should be judged on its own.

Pam was there with yet another in her ongoing string of rescued rottweilers, and Sula wandered over and began licking Pam's hands and legs, shyly trying to climb into her lap.

"She knows who she needs on her side," I said.

"I'll take her," Pam said, aghast at the words she was hearing from her own mouth. "If you really need me to."

So why didn't I leave her behind?

Simple answer: Because I couldn't bring myself to do it.

Because I didn't want to be always handing off my problems to other people in the end.

Because I wanted to know what became of her.

Because despite everything I knew to be true, I didn't even want to trust Pam with my little Sula's future.

Because all my efforts to avoid bonding with her had failed completely and I loved her. I loved her. I loved her in the end.

• • •

I had a room stacked full of boxes that I was trying to keep hidden from the dogs, to keep them from knowing what was going on—that we were leaving. Brando slipped in one day, and I found him burrowing his head into the bottom of one of the boxes. When he pulled his head out, he was holding in his mouth the small red collar he had worn when I had met him.

"Don't worry," I told him. "I won't forget to pack it."

A few days later, the rental truck had arrived, and I was trying to sneak things past the dogs so that they wouldn't become alarmed at the changes. Of course, it wasn't really possible, so at some point I broke down and brought them out to meet Tom, a student who had foolishly offered his assistance. Brando instantly loved him and wanted to join him in the back of the truck. I was ready to leave Tallahassee, but there had been a pit in my stomach anticipating how the dogs would take it, particularly Brando, who never wanted anything to change. He was stubborn sometimes about his friendships, as if there was a limit to the number of people he could trust or meet. Maybe if he trusted Tom, who was packing up all our things into a giant truck, Mississippi wouldn't be so bad.

One of the great drawbacks of dogs is that they don't help in the moving process at all, and one of the drawbacks of living on the semester schedule is that you are always moving at the one time no one is around. And I'm terrible at asking for help, so when people called and asked if they could come play with the dogs to say good-bye, it didn't occur to me that I should ask them to help carry anything. Actually, I think I thought they could distract the dogs while I got some of the work done. Janine called to say that she was driving up from Fort Lauderdale, and Pam and her husband came by with dog toys for Zephyr and Brando. Tom had a look of quiet confusion as they arrived one after the other, passed him heaving heavy boxes, and went directly into the yard.

The following morning Tom drove the truck, and I crated Sula in the back of the van and let Zephyr have the backseat to herself, while Brando rode shotgun. As we drove farther away from Tallahassee, in a direction he had never been, Brando stretched his head across the bucket seats and buried it in my lap.

I received three calls from strangers, one after the other, as we pulled into our new town. They were calling about Sula, whom they had seen listed on Pit Bull Rescue Central. They wanted to adopt her. They were in Florida. We were not.

"I could drive out and pick her up," one said, not understanding the process at all. I would want to know that Sula felt comfortable with them. That they liked her. I would want to see where she'd be kept. I was not trying to get rid of her—I was trying to find her a home.

• • •

The house we were renting—I can't help speaking in the plural, although the dogs were not chipping in—was a small square with a large living/dining room and two bedrooms off to the side. I had decided to make one of them a dog room, so that the living area could be kept normal. This didn't last long—at some point Sula began refusing to even step into the dog room because she understood that being walked in there meant I would be leaving. Instead, she would curl up on the couch and close her eyes, as if she could make me stay by playing dead. Eventually all the crates moved back into the living room, where I could keep her crated next to my desk as I worked.

When we first arrived, the landlord hadn't moved all his belongings out, and he had a few things around the house that still needed fixing. Brando hated him. So one day, while the landlord stayed working on the house, I took Brando to New Orleans. Before we left, I told the landlord to just leave the girls in their crates. They would be fine for the day, and that way he wouldn't have to keep track of them.

I knew as soon as we pulled away that the guy wouldn't listen to me. And I was right. We returned home to find that Sula and Zephyr had spent the day running together around the enormous overgrown backyard. Nothing terrible had happened. Maybe I was a little too controlling after all. So from then on, I let the dogs out together and watched as they played chase or grazed on the tall grass. The problem was that the yard was so large, at times I couldn't see them, and one night I lost them altogether in the darkness and shrubs. I could hear them, they were there somewhere, but they wouldn't come to me when I called. I walked around in the pitch-black darkness, trying not to panic, calling their names.

Inside the house, free to roam, Sula began to let her personality show. Even though she was fully grown now, she was still working out her lost puppyhood. She had an insatiable appetite for play and two dogs to choose from. When one was exhausted, she simply ran to the other. One afternoon Brando and Zephyr lay down in separate parts of the living room and pretended to be asleep so that they wouldn't have to play with her. Flabbergasted, Sula began tapping Brando with a paw and yipping at a painfully high pitch. When that didn't work, she grabbed his ear in her mouth and began tugging at it. He still kept "sleeping."

Pit bulls are great practical jokers. When Brando was younger he loved to steal things out of the pockets of people on the street. Once he even got a wallet. When I emerged from my shower one morning in Mississippi and found that my glasses had been stolen from the side of the tub, I could guess who had done it. "Sula?" I called, and she ran into the bathroom looking as if she had no idea why I was calling her, but there they were, lying in her spot in front of the TV.

Then, after a few weeks of freedom, Sula learned how to jump the fence, and she was gone. In the morning or late at night, she would leap unexpectedly over the fence and run down the railroad tracks. Often it seemed clear that she was waiting for the right moment, when I was too far to catch up and grab her, when she knew she could make it over without interference from me. I grabbed the flashlight and followed her into the night, watching as she occasionally peered over her shoulder at me and kept going. I kept a lasso on a shelf, and would literally have to sneak up close enough to toss the noose around her and rope her in.

I began to fear, more than anything, losing Sula. Literally losing her. This was ridiculous, I knew, and I felt guilty for allowing her to occupy my thoughts when she still wasn't really my dog. But Brando, who could easily slip over the fence, never thought of leaving, Zephyr had her hunting to keep her occupied, and Sula . . . liked to run free. I wondered who would find her, what would happen. I also began to wonder if this was how she came to me: not after being abandoned or used in a fight, but simply running away like a little adolescent maniac. The minutes I spent running after her in the darkness were filled with melodrama: How would I live with myself? When would I stop wondering where she was and whether or not she had found someone whom I hoped would treat her even better than I did? When eventually she let me catch up to her, I would ask her over and over on the way home: *Why are you trying to break my heart?*

There were clues sometimes that she understood the game: During the day, she would jump into a fenced-off vacant lot that opened into a yard on the intersecting street—I would run down, turn the corner, and cut through a stranger's yard as she made her way through the gate. One morning, as I made the turn, I saw that someone had bungeed the gate shut, so Sula was sitting, waiting for me, on the other side. Usually I didn't even have the leash with me, so I would pick her up and run home with her, surprised at how winded I would become running with a pit bull in my arms.

Even Zephyr started running away, burrowing under the house and out through the front, and then strolling down the busy avenue as if she were on her way to an appointment. Did they even understand, I wondered, the concept of the fence? Did they think that the world was just a large marble and that if they kept running forward they would find their way back again, into the yard, into the house, into the bed?

Every time I ran from the house after one of the girls, Brando stayed behind, wailing his high-pitched baby cry.

Eventually he began to cry even when we were all together, as if he was anticipating the inevitable separation that was coming.

I was exhausted. I was having dizzy spells, anxiety attacks. I was teaching and taking courses and on weekends traveling to do events for my previous book at fund-raisers and promotional events for rescue groups around the country. No wonder I was feeling overwhelmed. But I blamed the dogs, too: They expected too much, as if there was a competition among them for my attention, and just one of me was never enough for them.

Sula continued to get sick, and the vets couldn't tell me what it was. Vomiting, diarrhea, and extreme moodiness overcame her. She spent most of her time curled in a little ball, letting out small sighs. They ran test after test while I cleaned up puddles of vomit and bloody, tarry diarrhea. I e-mailed Debbie Geiger with news of each visit; she called the vet from hotel rooms in Switzerland to arrange payments. I was so convinced one night that Sula would die by morning, I let her come into the bedroom, and when she curled up on my jeans on the floor next the bed, I invited her up, where she slept the night resting her head next to mine on the pillow, snoring like crazy.

After almost two months of this, they finally had a diagnosis. She had *Giardia lamblia*, a nasty parasite that comes from drinking bad water. She probably lapped it up from a puddle on one of her runaway missions. But why had it taken two months and hundreds of dollars to diagnose when the treatment was the over-the-counter wormer Panacur?

Sula was well again, but she stayed in the bed, and with Sula in the bed, Zephyr joined us, so there was 220 pounds of dog sleeping with me: Brando, as always, at my feet, Zephyr in the middle, and Sula on the pillow. In the morning I woke up stiff, my limbs numb, as if I had been twisted so much that my body no longer had circulation. After years of waking up at five every morning, I found myself sleeping in, sometimes opening my eyes to find Zephyr sitting on my chest, staring impatiently down on me, and I would wonder how long she had been there.

One of the reasons we rescue things is to feel a sense of control that we may not really have in our own lives. If we can save something, maybe then we can do anything. Or maybe saving that one thing really is all we can do, but we will have done it, absolutely. Yet Sula seemed beyond saving. She wanted to be spoiled, and she wanted to run away. She was constantly under treatment, yet she was inevitably sick again. The more time I spent with her, the more bonded I was to her, and the more frustrated at the situation. I was convinced there was no point in adopting her out because she was so clearly going to die. Soon, I thought, even though I couldn't bear it.

But I was the one who was dying.

If I were a dog, my instincts would have let me know something was wrong sooner. Looking back, I am not sure how I could have been in so much denial. There were weekends when I slept for literally two days. "I slept like a dead man," I told people, not realizing it was true. I began to get dizzy, once even falling across the top of a dog crate while putting out food. I was out of breath, nearly always. The dogs, of course, knew something was wrong, and I chose to ignore them. It was just Brando crying, or Zephyr needing to sit on me to get me up in the morning. Sula began to leap on me while I was at my desk—not just climb into my lap, but seriously leap—and then she frantically licked my nose and ears and mouth while Zephyr poked me with her paw. I decided it was a respiratory infection and went to the clinic, where, after taking my pulse, they asked, "Is it always this low?"

"How low is it?"

"Twenty-five."

I could tell by the whispering outside the exam room door that something wasn't right, but aside from the fatigue I felt fine, so when the doctor returned and told me that I needed to go to the emergency room and that they were arranging for someone to drive, I asked, "Can't I just drive myself?"

And when, after being driven to the hospital, I was taken directly to the cardiac wing of the ER, I just thought that they had run out of room elsewhere. An orderly attached EKG equipment, and various staff members came by to stare at the screen without speaking to me. Occasionally someone would ask how I was feeling. "Fine," I said. "A little groggy."

"Really," they said, their voices rising in disbelief. On the EKG screen, my pulse was wavering between twenty and thirty. When no one was watching, I stared at the screen and whispered, "Go up! Go up!"

They attached large metal electrodes to my chest and said, "Don't worry, this is just in case." Finally someone came to explain it to me.

"Your heart has stopped working," he said. "Essentially it's stopped pumping on one side, and the other half has been trying to keep up."

"What does that mean?"

"It means you need a pacemaker."

"When?" I asked, thinking I could schedule some more convenient time.

"Now."

"You mean 'right now'?"

"Yes."

"Is there any chance that it will fix itself on its own?" For a moment, I wondered if it might be heartworms.

"No. It just happens sometimes for no reason." It's like an electrical short, like a toaster that suddenly only heats up on one side. All of the symptoms I had been feeling—the anxiety, the shortness of breath, the exhaustion—were caused by the fact that my heart had started shutting down months ago. Yet the treatment would be accomplished overnight—inserting a battery in my chest, threading a wire through the artery to my heart. It was absurdly much easier to treat than Sula's heartworms.

• • •

I had never been in a hospital overnight, and I had never been put under for any procedure, ever. But the dogs were my only conscious concern—because when it came down to it, they were the only thing I still controlled. I had left them just after breakfast that morning, thinking that I'd be home in an hour. I hadn't brought a cell phone.

When you bring animals into your life, there is one thing of which you can be fairly certain. They will die before you do. If you are like me, you plan on it, and get yourself a spare dog or two so that you won't, after that predictable tragedy, find yourself trying to replace a dog that you knew was irreplaceable from your very first meeting. The only thing that had prepared me for this moment was a long history of morbid daydreams of what would become of the dogs if something happened to me. I had actually pictured this scene: me on my deathbed in some dark and dingy hospital, spending one last moment with the dogs who had been smuggled in to see me before the end.

I remembered once asking my mother what she would do with the dogs if anything happened to me. "I'll try to find them good homes," she said matter-of-factly. I worried that it wasn't possible to find a good home for my three dogs, that they were too troubled for anyone other than me to take care of them.

By now a few friends had arrived in the ER and were standing alongside my bed as I tried to convince the hospital that it would be okay for them to let me go. I promised I would return within an hour. It was the same promise I had made—and broken—with my dogs that morning. There was something startling, and reassuring, about the fact that at this moment I was thinking of my dogs. How awful—how embarrassing—if my thoughts had been only of myself.

"We'll take care of it," Case said.

"But it would be easier if I just went home, took care of them, called the dogsitter, got my cell phone." I didn't just want to take care of them. I wanted to see them.

I asked for paper and a pen to write down the instructions for how to take care of my dogs, imaging a quick litany of likes and dislikes—how Brando likes to meet people first next to their car, because then he thinks someday they'll take him for a ride in it; how Zephyr only acts as if she doesn't need you there; how Sula likes to rearrange the dishes and bowls in her crate, sometimes putting one in each corner, sometimes stacking them—but the only thing I could think to write down was "1½ cups, twice a day." Was this really all there was to it? No, but I wanted to believe the doctors that I would be back home by morning.

"You should go and take Sula to the vet's office to stay. Just tell them what happened. Brando and Zephyr will be in their crates, but Brando will act like he's going to kill you. Just get Sula, and then see if you can find my dogsitter."

• • •

"Do you have family?" the nurse asked as she checked me into the room.

"Family?" I asked.

"Will someone be staying with you?"

I had talked to my parents on the phone, and we had agreed it was ridiculous for them to come down from Pennsylvania. According to the doctors, I would be back to normal by the time they arrived. But now I felt like an embarrassing failure. Apparently I was supposed to have family with me, and there was none. I couldn't answer her question; I started crying instead.

"It's okay to be scared," she said, taking my hand. "This is a scary thing."

• • •

On the operating table, as they prepared to knock me out, the surgeon asked what I did for a living. They were tying my hands to the table, so that I didn't "try to help out" during the operation.

"I write," I said. "I write about dogs."

"Oh," he said. "I have a dog. It's the best dog in the world." Then he looked across the table at one of the people assisting. "Didn't you just get a dog?" he said. "Yes," she said. "A puppy." "How's he doing?" "He's great." Soon everyone in the room was talking about their wonderful dog, their fantastic puppy. Soon I was gone.

When I opened my eyes there was aqua tenting covering my head. "What's up?" I asked. They were just closing me up. They opened the tent and I saw a woman with a laptop programming my new batteries as they glued my chest shut.

When they wheeled me back to my room, another friend, Travis, was there. Then Case joined him. Then Allison and Ben and Jay and Brit—all of them classmates I had known only a few months. Other people called or sent messages. I thought about the number of friends I have known who have been hospitalized, and how easy it is to think that to visit or call would be useless or intrusive, that it was best to wait and let them get well on their own. I was ashamed. I knew now that I would remember everyone who had visited that night, just as I would remember, in the weeks that followed, everyone who acted as if nothing had happened to me at all.

It's easier, when dealing with dogs or people, to think that our compassion isn't necessary—that it is someone else's duty, that someone else will come along.

That night, as I lay alone in my bed in the hospital, I thought back to the conversation in the operating room and felt sure that none of those people had a dog. I was convinced that they were telling me what they thought I wanted to hear, but as usual, I was wrong. Later, when I returned for follow-up appointments, each office I visited had a framed dog portrait on the desk.

• • •

The next morning, after a breakfast of bacon and eggs, I was allowed to go home. Brando and Zephyr scampered around me and then followed me to the couch, where they sat on either side of me, each licking one half of my face. Once I was appropriately drenched with their scent, Brando settled his head into my lap.

It's impossible to fully articulate what it means when your own heart fails you. Zephyr pressed her ear to my chest and left it there, pleased with herself, and pleased with what she was hearing, guarding it and reminding me that my heart couldn't be trusted. Because I wasn't supposed to move my left arm, I had to try to push her away with my right. She just settled in closer to my left side and pressed her ear closer to my heart. I was still sore from the surgery. My mind was still trying to catch up on what had happened. I didn't want a dog checking my heartbeat, reminding me of what was wrong. After an afternoon of struggling to keep her from me, I packed up her things and asked a friend to drive us up to the kennel, where Sula was staying alone. It would be better for everyone, Sula would have a friend, and Brando would be no trouble staying with me a few days at home.

With my heart beating again for the first time in months, all my senses were heightened. I hadn't realized how dull they had become. More than anything else, I was aware of the absence of Sula and Zephyr. Without them, I was reminded that something major had happened.

Brando stayed close to me, but every night after sundown he went outside to the back fence and howled into the distance.

dogs i reunited with their people

---

1. Francois was a yellow Lab whose name wasn't really Francois. I called him that because his long nose and worried expression made me think he'd look great in a beret. Francois was just a few months old, and after wandering the neighborhood he ended up sleeping in my neighbor's carport, where he cried all night beneath my window. The next day I took him in, and that night he slept quietly in Brando's crate after a flirtatious game in the yard with Zephyr, who tried to teach him how to dance. Francois was distracted though, probably thinking about his owners. We put an ad in the paper and waited for them to call.

2. One day in the middle of a storm I looked out the window and spotted Brazen in the middle of the street, cars swerving to miss her but never slowing down. I called her over and walked back to her house, where the front door was wide open but no one was around. I led her back to the yard, shut the gate, and called the police, who didn't find

anything suspicious inside, but questioned me about the dog, wondering how I got her back behind the fence. "She's a rottweiler!" they said. "Yeah," I answered. A few weeks later the neighbors told me, "When the police said that a neighbor had brought her home, we knew it must be you."

3. Driving across town in the middle of a growing storm, I tracked a German pointer as it zigzagged across the Florida State campus until I finally did the thing I'd always feared more than anything. I almost ran down a pedestrian in my effort to save a dog. Worse, when the woman raised her head and began swearing and gesturing at me, I realized it was the woman from the office next to mine. She recognized me, turned, and ran. After pulling the car over I caught up with the dog, and we waited out the storm under a bus stop awning. "Is that your dog?" someone asked. They seemed surprised that I would wait with it if it weren't mine. I called the vet listed on his tags and dropped him off once the storm was done. "He's afraid of thunder," they told me. "And his owner is completely deaf, so he never knows he's gone."

things that
return

My NEIGHBORS HAD A SMALL DOG—A DACHSHUND MIX—
whom one of their sons had found in Alabama while visiting a
"lady friend." I'm not sure why he brought her home to them—
they'd had several dogs before, according to my landlord, and
none of them lasted long. Now they had this little dog, not
much larger than my foot, and they kept her alone in their yard,
mostly, I think, because she was hyper and timid and fearful of
all but the one child in the family who took care of her. Like
Katrina, or any other dog, this nameless girl didn't understand
what she was doing alone in the yard. She got excited on the
rare occasions that any of the humans joined her and then
barked and yipped and crawled through the fence to get to
them once they were gone. Like Katrina, she began to notice
that my dogs got to play together, and with me, and she edged
her way closer to our side of the yard. All of my dog family were
in love with her, but none more than Sula, who would crane her
neck as soon as we went out the door, looking to see if her little girlfriend was there. Then I would take her, on a leash, over
to the neighbors' fence, where the two of them would run back
and forth bowing at each other.

After I returned from the hospital and sent the dogs away, the neighbor dog began to run right over to my house, jetting through the tall grass from one side of the yard to the other. She was looking, I thought, for the missing dogs. I picked her up and carried her over to her own house, knocked on the door, and waited for someone to come claim her. No one answered. I brought her back to my house, and a few minutes later I heard the neighbors' car pull out of the drive. They had been home, but just hadn't felt like dealing with the dog.

What to do about this dog—it was a question that had been on my mind for months. I knew that she was likely to run away, or that the family, who had ignored so many dogs before her, would get tired of her attempts to gain their attention. But they hadn't done anything abusive, so there wasn't anything for me to report.

I was still on pain pills and wasn't supposed to use my left arm. I had called my friend Case and asked him to come over to repair the back fence, so that once the girls returned I wouldn't have to worry about them escaping and I wouldn't have to worry about chasing them down with my faulty heart. When he arrived, the little dog and I were waiting for him. "Can you take us up to the shelter?" I asked.

"How many of those pills did you take?" he wondered. I explained that I was just going to drop off the dog, then let the neighbors know where to find her. I didn't want to have to watch over her, and I suspected they wouldn't care in the end.

I'd been to the shelter before. I'd offered to do a fundraiser for them, but they were too busy. This might seem strange, a cash-strapped organization turning down an opportunity for money, but it isn't that uncommon. Often they are so overwhelmed, so understaffed, that they can't even consider accepting help, or they fear that the offer will actually require from them work that they haven't the ability to do. As we drove up to the shelter, the little dog squatted and took a dump in the plastic cup holder between the truck's seats. Case looked at me, and we both tried not to say anything, until the smell got to be too much. "I'll clean it," I said.

I had taken animals to this shelter before, including another dachshund whom I'd found in the middle of an intersection on my way out of town several months earlier when my heart still didn't have a beat. That little dog had been part of a pair, but only one of them came into the car. The other ran away and hid. How do little dogs like this break free and end up on the lam? They can't, unless their owners aren't watching.

When I'd brought in that first dachshund, the staff at the shelter were having lunch and didn't want to be interrupted. In fact, they were among the rudest people I've ever had to deal with—and I used to live in New York. They sat eating their lunch, and finally one of the three decided to get up to take the dog. The intake form had no numbers for filing or tracing the animal, and when I asked how I could follow up on the case, they said, "Call and say you brought in a dachshund." What if there is more than one there? "There isn't." I had been planning on leaving a donation, but I got the sense they wanted me out of there as quickly as possible. It wasn't until I was on my way home that I realized I had forgotten to write a check. Sometime later I was speaking with one of the shelter's board members and mentioned the incident; suddenly I was on the phone with the shelter's director, who spent thirty minutes telling me that I needed to realize how hard they worked. I did, I said, but that didn't mean they should be so rude.

Now, with my neighbor's dog, Case and I sat waiting for their attention again. I asked if they had any paper towels or something I could use to clean up the mess in the car.

"No."

I went into the bathroom and got paper towels and found some disinfecting wipes.

Then they wanted to know where I had gotten the dog.

"You didn't just take it from the yard, did you?" they asked, scowling.

"I'm going to leave a note," I explained.

• • •

Back at home, I wrote:

Dear neighbors,

Your dog was out running in the street again today, and when I knocked on the door there was no answer. I just got out of the hospital and had to send my own dogs to stay somewhere else. I couldn't keep an eye on your dog and didn't want her to be run over, so I took her to the animal shelter. You can pick her up there. Let me know if you have any questions.

• • •

For the rest of the week Brando and I sat together on the couch, not watching television, just staring at the same empty space across the room from us. Finally I turned to him and said, "It's time for them to come home." I wasn't sure I was ready, but I couldn't take the silence anymore, and neither could Brando.

Zephyr and Sula raced each other out to the van, and both squeezed into the front seat with me for the drive home. They had spent the week playing together, and for several days afterward they continued to chase each other around our own yard, leaving Brando and me on the sidelines, which was where I belonged, at least for now.

Brando was awkward and shy around them, sensing that something had occurred between them that he hadn't been included in. And they must have sensed the same about us. At night I let them all climb into the bed with me: Sula at my pillow, Brando at my feet, and Zephyr at my side.

• • •

I began going up to the shelter every afternoon to check on my neighbors' dog, to make sure they didn't just put her to sleep. She was always thrilled to see me, and I would walk her around the yard and talk to her, letting her know she hadn't been forgotten. At least not by me. On Tuesdays from noon to two they euthanized the "unadoptables," and more than once I accidentally arrived just when they had finished. The doors of half the cages were hung open, empty and ready to be hosed down for the next occupant.

They had named the little dog Sue Ellen, and they were waiting to do a heartworm test before listing her as available for adoption. This was supposed to happen within five days, but they were, in their favorite word, "overwhelmed." The feeling I got was that they really didn't want anyone coming around, unless you were taking one of the dogs with you, in which case they seemed likely to give them up to nearly anyone. Each time I came to visit, they had moved her to a different location in the shelter; one day when I couldn't find her, they admitted they weren't sure where she was, either. "If you walk around a few times, she's out there somewhere," they said.

I offered to start a foster program, explaining that adoptable dogs could live in temporary homes and open up more spaces to save some of the dogs from being euthanized. They were not interested. "We don't put adoptable dogs to sleep," they said, and I realized, of course, they must divide them all into those two categories, because how could they live with themselves if they thought they had killed an adoptable pet?

I watched as the volunteers—most of whom seemed to be working off community service sentences—prepared the dogs for a cold winter night, spraying the cages with a hose without even letting the dogs out, then tossing a blanket in for them to make a nest. A few slots down from Sue Ellen there was a gorgeous, quiet rottweiler whose cage was labeled HOLD; then a few days later the HOLD designation was gone.

"What's the story with that rottweiler?" I asked.

"Heartworm," I was told.

"What will happen to him?"

"We can't adopt him if he has heartworm. It's a very complicated treatment."

Don't tell me about complicated treatment. They just didn't have the money to treat him. And they didn't have the time to call any rottweiler rescue groups. And maybe, just maybe, they didn't really care.

"So you're putting him to sleep?"

"Yeah." The woman was so cavalier about it, there was something almost gleeful lurking in her face.

I thought of Pam, and without actually asking her, I said, "I know someone who will take him." I wanted to take him out for a walk first, so that I knew what I was getting into. My own girl dogs were just back from the kennel, and Brando was waiting, like a good dog, for every routine part of our lives to return. I was on pain pills and still uncertain of what had happened to me and to my own heart. I opened the door to the rottweiler's kennel and lassoed him with a plastic leash. He was unsteady on his feet and didn't want to walk too far. There was poop in his fur, and I noticed that his blanket and bed were sitting on top of poop, as if they had been slid in on top of his mess—as if they didn't need to clean his cage, since he wasn't going to live long anyhow. He leaned against me and looked up into my eyes.

"It's fine you want to come up and walk him," one of the staff told me. "But you'd better do it off the property, because we don't know what his temperament is and we can't have him mauling a child or something."

"You mean he's been here a month and no one has ever walked him?"

"That's right," the woman said. There was a perverse degree of pride in her voice, as if she wanted to make clear that she didn't care what I thought of her.

There are ways to test a dog's temperament without ever taking him out of his cage—tapping his food with a broom handle, testing his response to quick movements or loud noise—but this dog hadn't even warranted that. Or they hadn't kept a record of it.

I e-mailed Pam and sent pictures. She said she'd take him, but not for a month. She had made actual vacation and holiday plans with her husband and for once she wanted to keep them without working another stray dog into the mix. I certainly wasn't going to argue with that thinking. I called the vet to see if they could board him for a while, and after some rearranging they managed to find room. Then Sula's sponsor offered to pay for the boarding—so the plan was set.

When I went up to get him, another of the shelter staff was working the desk. "He's such a good dog," she said. "I know the owners, and he's always been a good dog."

"You know the owners?" I said. I was stunned. If someone on the staff knew the dog's history, knew his previous owners, how was it possible that they didn't know his temperament? She told me that he had been owned by a female police officer in Detroit who brought the dog down to Mississippi to leave with her ailing mother. She thought the dog would take care of her mother, but the care of the dog was more than the woman could handle. He ran away, ended up in the shelter, and by the time they tracked him down the impounding fees were more than she could afford. I thought, if a person can't afford the impounding fees, she can't afford the dog.

"No, he's a good, good dog," she repeated. There were only three full-time staff at the shelter, and obviously they were too busy to speak to one another.

When I opened up the back of the van for the dog, he didn't want to go in. Or he didn't have the strength. His ribs were visible beneath the dull fur. I was hesitant to hoist him into the car myself, because he seemed so worried about his surroundings. "He likes women," the female staff person shouted from the porch, and she came out to lure him into the back. We closed the hatch and off we went.

His expression changed visibly as we drove past the shelter gates. He began panting and looking with interest at everything we passed. Then he took a dump. A big stinky dump. It was so bad even he didn't want to be near it, so he squeezed his way through the dog divider and climbed over the seat, and then into my lap. It was raining, the windows were fogged, and now there was a full-sized rottweiler blocking my vision. We nearly ran off the road.

"Get in the other seat," I said, but he didn't follow directions quite as well as Valentino had.

When we pulled into the vet's office he ran straight to the lobby, where he discovered staff that were, on that afternoon, all women. This thrilled him.

"Should we just file this under 'Rescue Rottie'?"

"Theo," I said. I don't know where the name came from, but now it was his.

It was a week before Christmas.

• • •

A month passed before I was able to get Theo out. During that time I visited him as often as I could. The vets told me that he had growled at another dog and they were worried that he might be aggressive. Actually, it wasn't the vet who said this, but a vet tech. At this particular office, it was rare that the vets spoke directly to their clientele, so the techs held the position of authority usually reserved for an actual doctor. They also made a lot of mistakes. On my first visit, after warning me that the dog might be aggressive, they had me visit with him alone while shut in a small windowless room. Theo dove play-fully between my legs. He sat for treats. And with each visit he was skinnier and skinnier. When I asked about this, I was told that he was eating well. "Maybe he needs to eat more, then," I said. "Well, we're giving him the recommended amount," I was told. "Isn't it strange, then, that he isn't getting better?" I asked.

I found out later that he was infested with worms and that his worming had never been completed in the month that we had paid for them to care for him. When I lived in New York, everyone compared vets, and everyone was usually looking for something better. Someone nicer, someone cheaper, someone who didn't overprescribe medication. I had a vet within walking distance of my apartment, and that was good enough for me at the time. Later, when I moved to Tallahassee, I found another vet within walking distance and realized what good vet care could be. They always found time to see a dog during an emer-gency, or even an imagined emergency. They weren't afraid of big dogs and actually were able to treat Brando more easily without me in the room. And they always offered discounts when I brought in stray animals.

But for the most part, we all deal with vets the way we deal with teachers and pediatricians. We want to believe that they are doing good, that they are doing the best they can, that they have our concerns in mind. Unfortunately, some of them are in it for the money. It takes a long time for any of us to give up on people we have put our trust in . . . but this vet in Hattiesburg had blown it as far as I was concerned.

My human friend Case was still talking about how I'd "stolen" the neighbors' dog. Despite my note, they didn't say anything to me for weeks, and then one day the father shouted across the lawn.

"Did you take that dog?"

"Um . . . yes I did."

"Well, you did us a favor," he said.

Their little dog, renamed Sue Ellen, did find a home. The shelter staff didn't have any other information than that. I took boxes of dog biscuits up to them as a thank-you, to show my support for what they had done, even though I didn't think they were doing enough. A few days later I went up to check on them again—the biscuits were still lying on the ground outside, where I had left them, untouched.

• • •

Case was going to Tallahassee to see his girlfriend, so we piled into the car with Theo and headed off. The plan was to get to Tallahassee by late afternoon, drop him at Pam's, drop Case at his girlfriend's house, then head to a party with a bunch of my old friends to celebrate the fact that I was still alive. Of course, everything went wrong. There were delays along the highway, so by the time we were approaching Tallahassee, Pam and her husband were getting ready to go to a dinner party themselves.

Actually, we were delayed because I was afraid of speeding. I was afraid of an accident. I was afraid of getting stopped with a strange rottweiler in the car.

Alternate plan: Get rid of Case and take Theo to my party. When I pulled into my friend's house, I took Theo out for a bathroom break and then knocked on the door to invite my friends out to meet him. Then he was back in the car for the rest of the night, while I ate pizza and told stories about my faulty heart.

Around midnight I drove back up to Pam's house, where we sat in the kitchen and talked for an hour. Not about my pacemaker or my heart, but about Theo and dogs. There was a line of crates along the wall of Pam's kitchen where she kept her foster dogs, and her own dogs were out in the living room, peering over the barricade. Once Theo settled into his crate, Sugar, the rottweiler who had "raised" Zephyr, came out to greet me and dance around me looking for affection. Now I knew where Zephyr got it from. While Pam accounted for the group of dogs she was fostering, and the group she had just adopted out, and the ones she was expecting in the coming weeks, I noticed the gnawed-off corners of the cabinets along the floor.

The next day I went up to visit again. I walked Theo around the grounds, where he wasn't fazed at all by the horses. He seemed to know what was going on—that he wasn't going back to a kennel. He leaned against me every few steps. Pam was busy with some people looking for a new dog, so I waited until they were gone before putting Theo in his crate on the back porch, where he could watch the horses. When it was time for me to leave, I considered heading straight to my car and letting Pam take care of everything from then on. I knew he was safe with her; she had received funding from a rottweiler club to pay for his heartworm treatment, and I knew from firsthand experience how picky she was about putting dogs into their final homes. But I had to see him again.

I walked back around to where he was relaxing in his crate. I don't think animals understand everything we say. *Peanut butter biscuit*, yes. *Walk*, yes. But I don't think they can understand the complexities of the way we articulate emotion. They can sense it, though, and they can sense our anxiety when we might feel that there is something we aren't telling them. I wanted to let him know that I was going, if only to make myself feel better about never seeing him again.

I leaned over his crate. "I'm going to go now," I said, and Theo stood and leaned toward me. "But you don't have to worry, because Pam is going to take care of everything." Theo licked my hands through the grid of the crate, and then my arms, and then I had to step away or else I was never leaving without him.

Dogs learn things through repetition; through repetition, I was getting better at good-byes.

• • •

The next morning, before I left town, I went back to my old neighborhood and visited Lisa and Bumpy for a few minutes before getting on the road home. Dusty the golden retriever had recently had a stroke but was back to normal, Lisa said. Bumpy sat next to me as Lisa gave me a going-away present that had been waiting to be sent all this time. I had been expecting something for the dogs, but it was a beautiful wood-covered journal for me to write in.

Across the street was my old house, and I looked out at it, surprised to see it from this perspective. When we'd left six months earlier, I had never imagined that I would return. But it wasn't my house anymore, really. There was no leaky hole in the roof. There was no Brando filling the huge space of the bay window. I stared at the small front porch, and the red door I would pass through every day, leaving Brando and the other dogs and then returning again.

Once, back when Katrina was still with us, I had come home in the evening and opened the back door for them to play before settling onto the couch with a magazine. As the light faded outside, I disappeared into the pages of some trashy, unimportant article and then was pulled out again by a faint knocking on the front door. If I had managed to read the whole article without being interrupted by a dog nose or a whine, something must be wrong. I remembered having opened the gate to the yard earlier in the day and realized the dogs must be gone. There was the faint sound of knocking on the door again, almost like a child uncertain of how it is done; it was Brando, who had run away but turned back again to see if I wanted to come along.

"Remember Katrina?" I asked Lisa. Of course she did.

I had been wondering all this time what might have happened to her, but was afraid to find out. What we want are happy endings. The trick is letting go of the idea that happy endings are based on what we hope instead of what we know.

"I tracked her down after I got out of the hospital," I said. I had e-mailed RUFF Rescue and held my breath waiting for their reply. Maybe she would have been better off if I hadn't opened my mouth that day, claiming I could take care of her, that I knew people who could find her a home. "She's living with a woman now. She's happy. She's doing well." I had found out another thing along the way: Katrina's mysterious benefactor had been the same as Sula's—Debbie Geiger had been helping us all this time.

It was a beautiful day, the sky clear and eternally blue. There was the urge to not rush anywhere, to just sit somewhere and enjoy it, but I had a long drive ahead of me and the dogs were waiting, I knew, for me to come home.

I thought of my missing heartbeat and Brando's blue ball. I thought of Sula's journey back here to where she was born; the red collar Brando wants to pack with us every time we move. There were a hundred things to think of on the long drive back: I thought of things that return.

how to
prepare for the
unexpected

Assume someday the worst will actually happen. Make a list of what you'll need. Think of the little things that you might forget on your way out the door: phone numbers, prescriptions, water, bowls, food, a leash for everyone.

Find out what your local evacuation plan is. Find out if they will rescue your pets with you, or whether you will have to choose to stay with them or leave them behind.

Make a list of people who you can rely on. Who can help you leave town. Who else might need help with their own family and animals? Who might welcome you and your dogs into their home?

Keep crates for each of your animals, even if you don't use them at home. If you find yourself having to live elsewhere, the hosts will appreciate it.

Make copies of important vet records. Get spare medicines—your pets' and your own. Take a minute to bring along the flea treatments and heartworm preventive, even if you are sure you'll be back in a day.

Don't assume a kindly vet will refill anything without an examination. Take everything that your dogs will need.

Keep your dogs' tags—including ID and contact info—on them at all times. Even if you don't plan to ever let them out of your sight. Remember that nature and bad luck sometimes interfere with our best intentions.

the
unexpected

———

THE DOGS AND I MOVED TO NEW ORLEANS IN THE SUMMER of 2005. On Piety Street, my first morning in our new home, I sat in the front room with the door open to the street, thinking that if I'd known what it would feel like to be surrounded by walls the color of pumpkin pie, I would have had the whole house done in that one color. But I had hedged, so the pumpkin pie front room was followed by a spice orange bedroom, a mayapple office, and spice orange again in the kitchen. The landlord hadn't finished yet with the bathroom, but pumpkin pie didn't seem like a bathroom color to me. It would have to be something light.

I was waiting for the television man to come and hook everything up. I had driven in from Hattiesburg, hoping that he would be late, and still I had the morning to sit looking out on my new street as a storm came and went, watching two women as they walked back and forth on the other side of the street. I had left the dogs behind in Hattiesburg for the day and felt guilty about it, even though my plan was to have everything ready for them when they came down a few days later. I wanted the first week to be for them with no other distractions as we settled in to the neighborhood.

I had lived in New Orleans ten years earlier and had planned to return ever since. When we moved to Mississippi, I began taking the dogs to visit the city, so that when we did move there, it wouldn't be foreign to them. They knew we had friends there. They knew the address of the Three Dog Bakery on Royal Street. Brando had even sniffed out the bookstore at Faulkner House in Pirates Alley, where he sought refuge from the carriage horses when he thought they were pursuing him down the street. Whenever I went to New Orleans on my own, Brando would recognize the smell on me and run to the door, expecting me to immediately take him with me and return. When I got a job teaching creative writing at NOCCA in the Bywater, along the river in the 9th Ward, the dogs joined me in celebrating.

It seemed too good when I found the house on Piety Street, a short walk from everything. I had been worried that I would never find a place in the neighborhood, within walking distance of my friends and the school where we taught. I was worried that there would be too many people ahead of me with better jobs. I was worried that the landlord wouldn't allow dogs. When he told me about his own dogs I asked "What kind?" He answered, "Rescued pit bulls," and I knew we were in. It probably helped that I had called all of my friends from the neighborhood, and as Mikey the landlord showed me around, they began arriving to check the place out with me. My friend Anne came from her house two blocks away with her new stepson Silas. "You have to take it," she told me as Silas stared out into the backyard, dense with banana trees and ginger plants. "What do you think, Silas?" she asked. He said, "I think it's amazing."

"What do I need to do if I want the place?" I asked.

"Nothing," the landlord said. "We don't need a lease."

Even when you live in a house in New Orleans, you spend all of your time on the street. My dogs understood this immediately—they couldn't have cared less that we had a backyard, since we were the only people who spent time there. They liked to head out the front door, down to the corner where retired drag queens and retired Navy men hung out at a card table in front of Frady's. These men were all so old and beaten down that it was hard to tell which of them was the drag queen. "My name is Steve," one of them said one day. "But you can call me Sharon. I prefer Sharon." Zephyr would flop onto her back and let one of the men tickle her with the stubs of missing fingers.

Or they'd go to the dog run, where Brando met and fell in love with a dog who looked just like him. "We should take a picture of them together someday," I said, and Grong Grong's parents, who were soon expecting a child of their own, agreed. On days when my dogs were particularly lucky, they would pass Anne's house just as she or her husband was leaving for work, and the dogs would rush to their sides fighting for the chance to lean on them.

• • •

I refuse to call the storm Katrina, although at the time I joked with Brando that it was our own Katrina, coming back to get us.

A week earlier, Grong Grong's dad and I had found a stray dog, a shepherd/Doberman mix who had come to the park on his own, his ribs showing, but thrilled to be around other dogs and people. When I offered to take him to the LA-SPCA, down the street along the industrial canal, Grong Grong's dad said that he might want to keep him. Grong Grong had come from the SPCA, too, and during the process of adopting him the shelter had been evacuated to Texas due to a hurricane threat and they had to wait, anxiously, for his return. Mr. Grong Grong was on his way to work. He found a spare rope in his car, and I walked home with Zephyr and the stray. The dog had a faded, illegible tag, but the SPCA would hold him until they determined if there was an owner. There would be a five-day waiting period. Then they could go and pick him up, so that Grong Grong would have a playmate before the baby came home.

We didn't know the hurricane was coming. We didn't know that by the time the waiting period was up, all of us would be gone.

• • •

That Saturday, a few days before the storm hit, I sat with a group of friends at Bacchanal, a wine cellar at the corner of Poland and Chartres, enjoying a free tasting of five Italian wines. No one was planning to leave the city. What we were planning was how to celebrate my and my friend Andy's birthdays. Her boyfriend was going to cook a Halal lamb that would be slaughtered the following week. The most anyone said of the storm was "I hope the lamb survives it." That and how if we missed classes on Monday, our lesson plans would be off by a day for the rest of the term.

Later that night a friend called to suggest I pick up an axe, so I could chop my way through the roof if I had to.

I began to think about the worst possible scenario. I could wade to higher ground, but I'd never be able to get my dogs out. Around 4 a.m. I found the flood map posted online. I called my friends to tell them I was leaving. But first I had to walk the dogs, down the street, past the dog park, where people were still debating whether or not to leave. As I prepared the dog's crates, the sun rose and the news anticipated an announcement from the mayor. Sula ran to the front door and threw it open with her paw, and then she disappeared. Outside, I spotted her racing toward the dog park, passing shrieking families loading their cars with children in strollers. In Hattiesburg, Sula had become accustomed to visiting the neighborhood children on her walks; it didn't seem to count as a walk if she didn't get to kiss at least one of them. I think it was the children that made her turn around, but instead of running to me, she ran across the street and headed toward St. Claude. There were men hammering boards to the front of buildings; men and hammers make Sula run fast. She kept running. I kept running. My heart surprised me and kept running. I saw her turn the corner and wondered if I'd be able to leave if I didn't find her. Finally she got tired, and I scooped her up into my arms.

I had heard that in Ivan people were trapped on the highway for twenty-four hours. I decided to go only as far as Hattiesburg, an hour inland from Biloxi. Jennifer, a former student who had just started her master's degree there, had e-mailed me that weekend, urging me to come up with the dogs if we needed a place to stay. Both sides of the highway had been opened up to evacuation traffic, and still it crept north slowly. I noticed how many cars were packed with nothing but pets. Reappearing on my right, I noticed two cars: a man in a pickup with a chow chow and a miniature pinscher followed by a woman in a hatchback with cages of parrots and other exotic birds. I assumed they were all traveling together. We were evacuating our pets, not ourselves.

• • •

Early the next morning, the electricity went out, and I watched as the sky flashed red in the distance. I had never seen anything like that before.

By noon the eye was above us, and we had drunk all of the wine. I lay down for a nap in the living room, while my host went with her cat into her bedroom. I opened my eyes to the sound of a huge gust of wind—before my nap the wind had already been bringing down the huge limbs of the oaks outside our windows. You expect a lot of sound, but the constant wind muffled everything, so one minute a tree was there, the next it was gone, as if it had never been standing at all.

I looked up at the closed bedroom door and saw it bump forward, as if there had been a burst of air behind it. Brando ran to the door just as my friend opened it from the other side. She was standing, quite still, with her cat in her arms. I leaned forward to pull Brando away and saw that her room was now filled with a tree—the trunk of an oak had plunged through the ceiling, shattered her television and most of the other components on her entertainment center, and narrowly missed her cat.

We spent the rest of the storm huddled on the living room floor. My dogs didn't even know there was a cat among them until the storm subsided. Everyone was still. My friend said she was worried that the rest of the tree would come crashing down on us. I pointed to the window and showed her that there wasn't anything left of the tree. When it was safe, I walked outside to check on friends down the street. Every couple of yards there was another whole tree or power line to climb over, every other house was at least partially destroyed.

We moved to another house later that night and spent the next days relying on friends and strangers who were cooking the contents of their freezers over fires. There was no electricity, no water, no phones, no TV, no information from the local authorities or federal government. The Red Cross spent most of Wednesday telling people they could get water at the Coca Cola plant—which proved to be completely untrue. There was no gasoline, and conflicting reports of which highways were passable and which were not drove us mad. The National Guard arrived with water and ice, but no one knew where they were distributing it. At least two people were shot in disagreements about ice. When we weren't out scavenging for information, the dogs were left inside, crated and panting in the heat.

• • •

When the refrigerators were empty, my friends began leaving town. At night, sleeping with the doors and windows open to escape the heat, I began to feel uncomfortable with the people wandering outside. There was no air-conditioning, and the heat index was above 100. I walked the dogs early in the morning and that was about it. In the afternoons I came home to find them panting, dehydrating, but there wasn't a lot of water, so I pulled them away from their bowl before they could finish it.

There was still no word on any help coming. I wasn't sure if the roads were clear or if we would find gas, so I loaded the car with dogs, the remaining dog food, some cans of spaghetti, and jugs of water that I had "purified" with Mountain Fresh bleach. The only way to leave was to prepare for the possibility that we would be stranded somewhere alone in the van. My phone began to work just out of town, and it was loaded with messages: people checking to see how they could help. I called Pam, and she and her husband mapped out a route. "If you run out of gas," she said, "let us know where you are, and someone will come to get you." In Meridian, just as the gas tank hit empty, we found a station that was open and waited in line for a few hours behind people who were hoarding tank after tank of gas. Then I stood in line at Wal-Mart waiting for a money transfer that never arrived. I worried that the dogs would be dead from the heat in the car when I returned, and I fed them Chicken McNuggets hoping they would forgive me. For everything.

When we arrived—eleven hours later—at my friend's place in downtown Atlanta, Zephyr ran out of the van into the street. I caught her just as my friends came down from their loft. Everyone took a dog and began walking them. To Sula this must have seemed like a carjacking. She broke free and ran down the street to me and Brando, leapt at me, and the next thing I knew the two of them were in a fight, locked onto each other's faces. They wouldn't let go. After all of this, I thought, now we're going to die. We'll kill each other. Zephyr, already down the street with her walker, turned back at the sound of the fight. Finally they let go, with barely a mark on either of them. That's when I began to hyperventilate and collapsed on the street.

My friends had planned a celebration for that night. It was my birthday, and I had forgotten. It was clear my dogs and I were a mess, so we sat quietly that night before opening the presents: dog biscuits, toiletries, and two sets of clothes for me to finally change into. We spent two days hiding out there and then headed to Tallahassee, where I had an old bank account that I would be able to access, and Case and his girlfriend Kathy had offered a place to stay. And Zephyr's Pam.

• • •

This is what I left with: three dog crates, three dogs, a bag of dog food, a single change of clothes, two bottles of wine. I didn't want to take too much, since it would only be a day or two that I was gone.

This is what I left behind: dog bowls, all of my photographs, all of my books, my iPod, my hard drive, my DVD collection, my pacemaker monitor, my health insurance cards, my bank cards, my checkbook, my clothes, drafts of stories, notebooks, packaged food that I would later want when I was hungry, bottled water, my address, my job, my students, my neighbors, my friends. Almost everything.

You think about whether you'll ever see your things again. You think about whether you'll ever go home. You think about the people you knew but didn't know, like Grong Grong and his family, their baby, and the stray dog we found that they were going to take home.

I had friends. I had people willing to make room for me and my dogs. I had more help than I knew what to do with, partly because it is hard to know what help you need when you don't even know where to begin. "I don't know if I need anything," I said when people offered to help. I didn't know how homeless I was. I didn't know what would help. I knew that there were plenty of other people and animals who needed more than we did. My friend Leslie Pietrzyk told me in an e-mail:

> After my husband died, all these people kept wanting to do nice things for me, and it was confusing, and I couldn't quite trust them or know why they were acting that way. Made me feel odd. Eventually, I decided that they were mostly doing things to make themselves feel better . . . so I let them, which is harder than it sounds.

The dogs knew this already.

Yet no matter how good my friends were, they could never really understand. When something this big happens—someone dies or you almost die yourself or you sit helpless and watch as the entire world seems to collapse around you—it completely rearranges you, from the inside out. All of the same pieces are there, but they have been put together in a way that only you can sense. People look at you, recognize you, and you have this secret that you can never share with them. They'll never completely understand that you've become an entirely different person. The person they think they know is gone.

Case and Kathy had cats that moved into the bedroom when we arrived. Brando's crate was positioned in the dining room. I slept on the futon in the living room. Zephyr and Sula spent nearly all of their time crated in the office in the back of the house. Zephyr was getting sick, struggling to go to the bathroom, alternately constipated and suffering from diarrhea. One night, checking on her and Sula just before bed, I looked down at her and recognized something behind her eyes. She looked shrunken, as if her fur didn't quite fit her anymore. She had been rearranged on the inside, too. Sitting back there all week, she hadn't been able to do the thing she had devoted her life to: keeping track of Brando and me.

There wasn't room to move the futon into the room with them, so I arranged the blankets and pillows in the space that remained between the desk and the girls' crates before bringing Brando into the room. We had never slept this way before, but he curled up immediately along the side of the blanketed floor. We slept that way all night, the four of us, each facing the center, facing each other.

epilogue

———

WHEN CATASTROPHE STRIKES, PEOPLE DIVIDE THEMSELVES pretty quickly into two groups. There are the people who stand back and ask questions—in this case: Why did they live there? Why didn't they leave sooner? Why didn't they know how to swim? The primary concern among this group is preserving the illusion that nothing this bad could ever happen to them.

And then there are the people who jump in. They raise money. They send clothes. They take people—and animals—in. While we were staying in Tallahassee, I got a call from Bob Shacochis and his wife Catfish, offering the keys to their vacant house for me and the dogs to move in. I didn't know them well enough to expect anything like this, but I knew them well enough to know this was the kind of thing they did. Still, I couldn't answer him on the phone. The words couldn't come. "Can I call you back?" I asked.

For five weeks the dogs and I stayed there, mostly sitting in the living room, watching the news, surfing the Internet, sitting on hold with FEMA—mostly just trying to occupy our heads with something, until night came and we could forget everything again. There was a large yard for Zephyr to chase squirrels in, and it opened into a public park. Sula was fascinated by the idea that we could leave through the front of the house, go for a long walk, and enter through this secret passage back into the house again. She wanted to do it again and again. There was a basket of dog toys, which Brando sorted through, tossing them into various, specific piles.

It was a wonderful home, but it wasn't ours.

So we returned. This time I was prepared. I found room for: sixty pounds of dog food, twenty-five gallons of water, a Coleman stove, six propane tanks, three boxes of groceries, a large air purifier, a respirator, a couple of gallons of bleach, rubber gloves, hand sanitizer, and Vicks VapoRub (to cut the stench). I had studied the flood maps. It looked like the water had reached our street, but hadn't risen high enough to get in. But I wasn't sure and I couldn't expect that there would be running water, electricity, gas, or open stores to get anything once we got in.

Brando sensed it as soon as we crossed into Mississippi. He was riding shotgun, and he rose onto all four legs, pointed his nose forward, and bowed his head. He didn't like what he smelled. I was worried I wouldn't be prepared for what I might see. But it was nothing. Literally nothing. Things grew worse as we approached the city: houses lay in ruins where I hadn't known there were houses before. They hadn't been there—they had traveled to their new locations on the force of the storm.

As we pulled into the city itself, I could see the brown waterline on the houses, and watched as the line lowered to nothing as we drove closer to the river and our home. Abandoned cars littered the streets, and stray city buses were parked haphazardly in the grass medians known as neutral ground, next to small boats anchored to trees. Sula and Zephyr wanted to head directly into the house, but Brando wanted to investigate the neighborhood. Three blocks north, on St. Claude, only my bank was left on a block that had mysteriously burned to the ground. Two blocks in the other direction, a warehouse, filled with small propane tanks, had burned down, sending the tanks like rockets through the area. The air was still filled with the smell of fuel and incinerated cement; Brando and I recognized it as the smell of 9/11. To the east, the SPCA shelter had been flooded and destroyed.

But we were lucky. Inside the house I found a small hole in the roof, and dried up trails of ash from the force of the rain coming down through the chimneys. Aside from that, it seemed everything was exactly as we had left it. A stack of unpaid bills. An unfinished book next to the bathtub. But rats had climbed up from the water while we were gone—they had gotten into the food and my clothes, they had gotten into things you wouldn't imagine even rats being interested in, except maybe with nothing else around. Electricity was restored to parts of the city, but went out again anytime rain fell, or if there was a gust of wind.

But we were lucky to be able to come back at all.

The rest of the neighborhood was still mostly uninhabited, although slowly people reappeared, one at a time: the old drag queen, the fingerless man. Mostly there were military, patrolling the area with guns. Packs of dogs had formed, and when I walked mine, early in the morning, we had to be cautious, not knowing when a trail of dogs might stampede by on the heels of one of the neighborhood cats. Not far from our own, a small female—an improbable mix of rottweiler and corgi—had staked out a home. She kept a close watch, but never approached and never let us come near. Within a few days, two other dogs had joined her, and then suddenly they were gone.

Three weeks later, she returned. Now she had a collar and again she was alone. When I walked Brando or Sula, she would run into the distance, but if she saw Zephyr with me, she would sit flat on the ground and wait. And that is how I lured her: with Zephyr and a handful of treats. I sat her on my lap and drove across the Mississippi, where the SPCA was holding animals temporarily in large heated tents—the kind you see pitched in a neighbor's yard for a wedding. In the aftermath of the storm, they had rescued over 8,500 animals. Sixty-two percent were pit bulls. Each day I drove back to help open mail—their staff was homeless and displaced too—and to walk into the tent and check on the dog. Eventually they would need to send her elsewhere, to another shelter, wherever in the country they could find room.

I was on the other side of town, sitting on my bumper, locked out of my van, waiting for a locksmith to come, when I got the call. She and eight other dogs had a ride out of town to a shelter in Ohio. I was a few hours away from finding out—via e-mail—that I was unemployed. It was about to start raining again. Another blackout was sure to occur. But for that one moment, all of the world's uncertainties seemed to rest on the shoulders of that one dog. I wanted to see her. I wanted to talk to the men who were taking her away. I wanted to know exactly whom she would ultimately live with, and whether she would be allowed to sleep on the furniture and what they would feed her. But there wasn't any logical way for me to discern those things that afternoon. I needed to allow that to be okay.

She would start a new life, in Ohio, where she would be named Jambalaya. And I would get into my car and drive home again, where my own dogs were waiting for me to return.

December 2005

what to do
when you find a dog

1. Don't chase him.

2. Call animal control if you can't get him yourself.

3. Try to find the owner: Check for tags, place an ad, make flyers.

4. Contact your local vets, rescue groups, or shelters.

5. Take the dog to the vet before allowing him to interact with your own animals.

6. Consider what you will do if you can't place the animal elsewhere.

questions for discussion

1. Ken Foster says that he wrote *The Dogs Who Found Me* from a position of not knowing what he was doing but choosing to do something anyway. How did that make you feel as you read the book? When have you taken action in your own life without knowing the answers?

2. There aren't many human characters in this book, and when they do appear, they are often on the sidelines. But there are a lot of dogs; which were your favorites and how did the author distinguish them from each other?

3. There are a number of tragedies in the book, from the attacks of 9/11, to the loss of a friend and the tragedy of Katrina. How do you think these events helped shape the author's outlook on life and the lives of animals?

4. The short chapter titled "How to Let Go" is about letting a foster dog move on to a new home, but it might be about accepting any number of changes that occur in our lives. How did this section, or any other parts of the book, speak to something more than just the story of stray dogs?

5. In the final chapter, Foster writes: "When something this big happens—someone dies or you almost die yourself or you sit helpless and watch as the entire world seems to collapse around you—it completely rearranges you, from the inside out. All of the same pieces are there, but they have been put together in a way that only you can sense. People

look at you, recognize you, and you have this secret that you can never share with them. They'll never completely understand that you've become an entirely different person. The person they think they know is gone." How did this make you feel, and what did it remind you of from your own life?

resources

In the first edition of this book, I offered a resource section that quickly went out of date. Rescue organizations closed down, missions changed, philosophies evolved. Here, finally, is an update. The real usefulness of these lists is as a starting point for people who want to learn more about animals, our relationships with them, and rescue. I've tried to include a range of organizations, but it is by no means exhaustive. There are many others to discover. I also must add that my listed things here are not meant as an endorsement. Each of these resources offer its own perspectives, sometimes in agreement with each other and sometimes not, but always worth considering.

—*Ken Foster*

BOOKS

Writing a good dog book is hard work—and there are a plenty of them out there. Here are a few that stood out to me in recent years.

Pit Bull: The Battle over an American Icon by **Bronwen Dickey**
A big, well-researched look at the breed and the people who love and hate it.

The Culture Clash: A Revolutionary New Way to Understanding the Relationship between Humans and Domestic Dogs by **Jean Donaldson**
A classic text regarding dog behavior and training.

Off the Leash: A Year at the Dog Park by **Matthew Gilbert**
A sweet memoir about falling in love with dogs and the community that owns them.

The Lost Dogs: Michael Vick's Dogs and Their Tale of Rescue and Redemption by **Jim Gorant**
The story of Michael Vick's dogs.

You Had Me at Woof: How Dogs Taught Me the Secrets of Happiness by **Julie Klam**
A humorous look at the world of dog rescue.

Inside of a Dog: What Dogs See, Smell, and Know by **Alexandra Horowitz**
A look at dogs from the inside out.

The Secret History of Kindness: Learning From How Dogs Learn by **Melissa Holbrook Pierson**
Lessons in human behavior found in the science of training dogs.

BEHAVIOR AND ADVOCACY
Here are just a few websites that offer great information on effective advocacy on behalf of animals, from dealing with compassion fatigue to managing behavior issues.

KC Dog Blog
http://btoellner.typepad.com/kcdogblog
Brent Toellner covers everything from news stories to welfare trends in his addictive blog, and he is able to apply logic to

pinpoint what is really happening beneath the slogans and statistics being shared.

Jessica Dolce

jessicadolce.com

Jessica Dolce's website offers information on dealing with compassion fatigue and rescue burnout, as well as links to her smart,
funny blogs: DINOS: Dogs in Need of Space and Notes from
a Dog Walker.

Sophia Yin

drsophiayin.com

Dr. Sophia Yin was a remarkably compassionate veterinary
behaviorist whose work and advice is preserved at this website.

Patricia McConnell

www.patriciamcconnell.com

Good dog trainers are hard to find, but Patricia McConnell's
pamphlets and books can help make sense of dog behaviors that
we may think are unique to our own dog.

ORGANIZATIONS

There are so many great organizations it would be impossible to
list them all, but this list is a start. I've added a few notes for
each of them, focusing on particular programs that make them
unique.

Animal Care Centers of NYC

www.nycacc.org

A nonprofit contracted to provide animal control and sheltering
services in all five boroughs of New York City, this organization

is the only "open-admission" shelter in the city, taking in over 30,000 animals annually regardless of their condition. It has in recent years reduced the number of abandoned animals and increased adoptions and placement of homeless pets to nearly 90 percent.

Animal Farm Foundation
www.animalfarmfoundation.org
Although its mission is to advocate for equal treatment of "pit bull" type dogs, many of its resources and grants are not breed specific.

ASPCA
www.aspca.org
The American Society for the Prevention of Cruelty to Animals (ASPCA) is not associated with your local SPCA, although the national group does work on programs that benefit animals and animal welfare organizations.

BAD RAP
www.badrap.org
Its name originally stood for Bay Area Doglovers Responsible About Pitbulls, but over the years its advocacy and grassroots community outreach programs have benefited dogs of all breeds.

BARC
www.barcshelter.org
An independent shelter in Brooklyn—Brooklyn Animal Resource Coalition (BARC) rescued my Brando and then changed my life by allowing me to adopt him.

Best Friends

bestfriends.org

Although its roots can be traced to New Orleans, Best Friends is a sanctuary located in Utah that has an increasing influence on independent rescue groups across the country through its annual conferences.

Downtown Dog Rescue

www.downtowndogrescue.org

This Los Angeles-based organization works with families to keep dogs in homes by offering resources such as food, training, and other tools. Founder Lori Weise's book, *First Home, Forever Home: How to Start and Run a Shelter Intervention Program,* offers tips on shelter intervention.

Found Animals Foundation

www.foundanimals.org

Focused on keeping animals in homes, Found Animals offers a microchip registry, low-cost chips, and other programs.

HeARTsspeak

http://heartsspeak.org

This amazing network of artists provides services pro bono to animal welfare organizations, offering everything from photography workshops to design services.

The Humane Society of the United States

www.humanesociety.org

Although a target for controversy, The Humane Society of the United States (HSUS) supports a number of great programs throughout the country, and its Pets for Life program and online toolkit offers a great blueprint for doing community outreach programs to pet owners in your own town.

KC Pet Project

kcpetproject.org

Many communities have wished they had control of their local animal shelter. The KC Pet Project actually did take over, responsibly, and brought a number of life- and cost-saving programs to its animal control system.

Leon County Humane Society

www.lchs.info

An example of the many independent humane organizations around the country, this group in Tallahassee, Florida, is where I found my own Zephyr.

Louisiana SPCA

www.la-spca.org

For more than a century, the Louisiana SPCA has helped animals and their owners in the New Orleans area. After Hurricane Katrina, it rebuilt a state-of-the-art shelter and education center and implemented a number of progressive community programs.

National Canine Research Council

www.nationalcanineresearchcouncil.com

The National Canine Research Council (NCRC) offers comprehensive, science-based research on dog bites, visual breed identification, and breed-specific legislation, along with free tools to achieve safe, humane communities.

No Kill Nation

www.thenokillnation.org

No Kill Nation is a national advocacy organization that helps communities achieve lower euthanasia rates by taking real action to help lower shelter intake and help place animals in homes.

Our Pack

www.ourpack.org

This organization has branched out from pit bulls to Chihuahuas in recent years, demonstrating how fad breeds on both sides of the size scale are often left abandoned.

Safe Humane Chicago

www.safehumanechicago.org

This organization manages a remarkable range of outreach and educational programs working with inner-city high school students and incarcerated youth, and a model Court Case Dogs program that gives volunteers the opportunity to help seized dogs that were victims of neglect.

MEDICAL INFORMATION

American Heartworm Society

www.heartwormsociety.org

The American Heartworm Society provides everything you ever wanted to know about heartworm disease, including maps, life cycles, and proper treatment for affected dogs.

Ark Sciences

www.arksciences.com

Ark Sciences is a nonprofit veterinary science company whose mission is to reduce pet overpopulation through alternative, non-surgical sterilizations. This quick, inexpensive procedure makes sterilization available to populations that previously did not have access to traditional methods.

Mar Vista Animal Medical Center Pet Web Libraries

www.marvistavet.com

This Los Angeles veterinary practice has a great website with information on medical conditions, surgical procedures, and pet medications.

Food

In the past decade, pet owners have been given an ever-increasing number of "premium" choices for feeding their pets on a variety of budgets. But what really matters in your dog's food, and how can you tell the truth behind the marketing? One easy method is to start reading and comparing labels—ingredients listed according to weight. There are also a number of websites that offer analysis of ingredients in each food. But be aware: formulas change over the years, and ultimately what matters most is what works for your individual pet.

The Dog Food Advisor

www.dogfoodadvisor.com

acknowledgments

When I began writing this book, I had what I thought was a novel idea: write only about the dogs and leave people on the sidelines completely. I quickly discovered that this was impossible. To tell the dogs' stories—or even my own—required a cast of humans. Which is as it should be. But there wasn't room for everyone, so I hope to fit them in here:

Ann Treistman, and everyone at The Lyons Press.

In New York: Sharyn Rosenblum, Ben Neihart, Terese Svoboda, BARC, Stacey Alldredge, Catherine Texier, Emily Twomey and Jamie, Garrett Rosso, Java, Jill Bossert, and everyone at the dog run. Well, almost everyone.

In Florida: Lisa Collins, Debbie Geiger, Pam Houmere, Cynie Cory, Tom Kay, Jennifer Westfield, Jeremiah Tash, Victoria Winterling, Bob and Catfish, Lisa Lambert, Mark Winegardner, Jimmy Kimbrell, Spurgeon and Sandy, James and Gaelynn, Trish and Eric Hanson, Liz Joyner, Janeen Wallace, Bridgitte Byrd, Westwood Animal Hospital, Kathy Connor, Judy Suplee, and Case Miller.

In Mississippi: Everyone at the Southern Heart Center and the Center for Writers, particularly Rick Barthelme, Steve, Angela, Rie, and Melanie; Martina Sciolino, Allison Campbell, Travis Kurowski, Jay Todd, Ben Butler, Britt Haraway, and Case Miller.

In Louisiana: the Louisiana SPCA, Faulkner House, Anne Gisleson, Brad Benischek, Silas, Julia Lane, Brad Richard, Andy Young, Deborah Choate, Lisa Robinson, and Case Miller.

Thanks also to the PEN American Writers Fund, the New York Foundation for the Arts, and the Wesleyan Writers conference. And my family.